Presented to

....

By

....

Date

....

Jessie Fioritto

BIG
PRAYER

180 DEVOTIONS FOR KIDS

BARBOUR **kidz**

A Division of Barbour Publishing

© 2022 by Barbour Publishing, Inc.

ISBN 978-1-63609-353-6

Published by Barbour Publishing, Inc., 1810 Barbour Drive, Uhrichsville, Ohio 44683, www.barbourbooks.com

Our mission is to inspire the world with the life-changing message of the Bible.

Printed in the United States of America.

001338 0722 BP

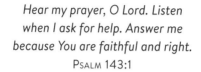

*Hear my prayer, O Lord. Listen
when I ask for help. Answer me
because You are faithful and right.*
PSALM 143:1

- - - - - - - - - - - - - - - - - -

Did you know that you have a powerful friend who's willing to listen anytime you want to chat? You can talk to the living God of this universe! And He wants to hear from you. He's ready 24-7. And not only will He listen, but He's so powerful that He can change your life! He can handle anything that's happening to you or in this wide world—just tell Him about it. You can trust Him because He's proved that He will never fail you. God says in the Bible, "Call to Me, and I will answer you" (Jeremiah 33:3). Talk to Him right now, and see what amazing things He has to say! He's waiting for big prayers from you.

God Hears Me!

*Hear my prayer, O Lord. Listen
when I ask for help. Answer me
because You are faithful and right.*

Psalm 143:1

Who do you turn to when you need help? Your mom or dad? A friend? Maybe a grandparent? But did you know that you have a powerful friend who will listen and help you anytime you ask? The God of the universe, the One who just speaks and amazing things happen—like creating our whole planet out of nothing!—is never too busy for you. And there's no problem too big for Him. So talk to Him today. He can't wait to hear from you.

*Heavenly Father, I could use some help. It makes
me feel happy and safe to know that I can talk to You
about anything that I'm having problems with, and
You are faithful to hear me and powerful enough to
help me with every struggle. And I can talk to You
anywhere, anytime. Today I could really use Your help
with _____. Thank You, God. Amen.*

Promise to Listen

"Then you will call upon Me and come and pray to Me, and I will listen to you."

JEREMIAH 29:12

- -

Have you ever wanted to talk to your friend about something really exciting or maybe something that was bothering you, but you could tell that your friend wasn't really listening to you? You've probably done that a few times too. It can be hard not to get distracted, even when you really care about your friend. But God wants you to know that He's never distracted. Even though He's the God of everything, He promises to listen when you speak to Him. You're that important to Him! And He loves you so much that He wants to hear every word you have to say. Spend some time talking with Him. He's listening.

God, I'm so glad to know that You hear every word I say to You. And You care about me and what's happening in my life so much that You want me to tell You about it. Today I want to tell You about _____. In Jesus' name, amen.

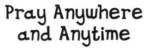

Pray Anywhere and Anytime

The Lord is near to all who call on Him.
PSALM 145:18

- -

I bet your mom and dad probably tell you to say your bedtime prayers. Maybe you even pray with your family to thank God for every meal. But prayer is simply talking to God. And the exciting news is that you can do that anywhere at any time! You shouldn't pray just because you feel like you'll upset God if you don't thank Him for your food. Don't forget that God loves you! He's your heavenly Father. He wants you to talk with Him all the time about all your joys and problems. You can talk to Him while you're walking to school or riding in the car to the store. You can talk to Him while you're alone or in a crowded room. There's no wrong place to pray. Try it right now!

Heavenly Father, thank You for always being there, no matter where I am. Today I want to tell You about _____. In Jesus' name, amen.

Ask the King

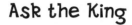

On His coat and on His leg is the name written,
"KING OF KINGS AND LORD OF LORDS."
REVELATION 19:16

- - - - - - - - - - - - - - - - - - - -

Who do you turn to when you have a problem? Probably someone with the power to help you fix it, right? You might ask a teacher for help when you don't understand your math, or you might go to a police officer if you get lost. The Bible tells us that we have access to the King of kings and Lord of lords (that's a pretty impressive title, right?). God is big enough to handle all your problems. This world can be ugly, and maybe you've gone through some very hard things. Talk to God about how you're feeling and the help that you need. He may not take away the hard times, but He can give you strength and teach you to trust Him through difficult experiences.

Heavenly Father, You are the King over all.
I trust that You love me and want what's best
for me. Today I'm having a hard time with
_____. In Jesus' name, amen.

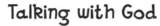

Talking with God

"And it will be before they call, I will answer.
While they are still speaking, I will hear."
Isaiah 65:24

- -

Prayer is talking to God. You probably talk to your parents all the time. You ask them questions and tell them about your day, and you listen when they talk to you. Listening is how you find out what they want to teach you, when they're proud of you, or when you need some instruction. They can also tell you that they love you. God wants this two-way conversation with you too! He wants to hear your questions, your struggles, and your joys. But don't forget that talking with Him also means listening for His answers. God speaks through the Bible. Take some time each day to read your Bible and pray for God to talk to you.

God, I'm so in awe of the fact that I can talk to You and You'll listen to me and have things to say to me as well. Today I want to tell You about _____. Amen.

No Fancy Words Needed

"When you pray, do not say the same thing over and over again making long prayers like the people who do not know God. They think they are heard because their prayers are long."

MATTHEW 6:7

- - - - - - - - - - - - - - - - -

Some people seem to have all the right words when they pray. But don't be intimidated by their public-speaking skills. God wants to hear from you in your own words. Stringing together fancy words won't make your prayer any more special to God. He cares about how you feel and what you're learning about Him. He wants a real relationship with you, not a fake one where you try to sound important. He doesn't want you to try to impress people with flowery prayers. He just wants to talk to you.

Lord, keep my prayers humble. I don't need to impress others with big words and long prayers. I just want to talk to You about _____. In Jesus' name, amen.

Help with Your Feelings

How long, O Lord? Will You forget me forever?
. . . Look on me and answer, O Lord, my God.
Give light to my eyes. . . . But I have trusted
in Your loving-kindness. . . . I will sing to the
Lord, because He has been good to me.
PSALM 13:1, 3, 5–6

Sometimes our feelings take us through some serious ups and downs. Sometimes you might feel like you're on top of the world, but at other times things go wrong and you might think God doesn't care about you. Do these feelings mean that God loves you less or that you can't talk to Him in prayer? No! Even David—giant-slayer and king of Israel—felt sad. He even asked God if He would forget him forever. But then David asked God to help him see the truth. And in the end, David chose to trust God's goodness.

God, I'm so glad that You listen to me even when I'm upset. Thank You for showing me the truth of Your love even when I feel down. In Jesus' name, amen.

He Knows Your Thoughts

You know when I sit down and when I get up.
You understand my thoughts from far away.
PSALM 139:2

- -

God knows everything about you, even your thoughts! That can be a little scary if you're thinking about things that you know He wouldn't like. But it's also comforting to know that He can hear all your prayers, even the silent ones. You don't have to talk out loud to have a conversation with God. You can pray at any time just by thinking it in your mind, and He'll be listening. It's pretty amazing to realize that the God who loves you is so powerful that He has the superpower of reading your thoughts. And because of this, you really can pray all the time.

Heavenly Father, I love that I can talk to You whenever I need to, even if I just think the words in my mind. You love me so much that You hear everything. Today I want to talk to You about _____. Amen.

Morning Prayers

In the morning, O Lord, You will hear my voice. In the morning I will lay my prayers before You and will look up.

PSALM 5:3

What's your morning routine like? You probably wake up to a buzzing alarm, brush your teeth, comb your hair, and pick out your clothes. Maybe you even make your bed. If you don't already, try talking to God in the morning too. Tell Him about your worries and fears for the day, ask Him what things He'd like you to do that day, and praise Him for the day He's given you. Begin your day thanking Him for the blessings you see around you.

God, good morning! Thank You for this day and this life You've given me to live. Show me what You want me to do today. Keep me from falling into temptations, and help me be a light for You. And please help me with _____. In Jesus' name, amen.

Big Plans

" 'For I know the plans I have for you,' says the Lord, 'plans for well-being and not for trouble, to give you a future and a hope. Then you will call upon Me and come and pray to Me, and I will listen to you.' "
JEREMIAH 29:11–12

- - - - - - - - - - - - - - - - - - -

It's easy to feel small in this big, crowded world. You might even wonder if anyone even notices you. But God knows you. He created you to be just who you are. He designed your looks and your personality—all so you could be part of His plan. He loves you so much that He sent His Son, Jesus, to die on the cross for your sins so you could be part of His family forever. God has special plans for you.

Heavenly Father, I want to have a future with You forever in heaven. And it makes me feel so happy to know that not only do You see me and care about me, but You've made me for a purpose. Please show me what You want me to do. In Jesus' name, amen.

Pray about Your Problems

So put away all pride from yourselves. You are standing under the powerful hand of God. At the right time He will lift you up. Give all your worries to Him because He cares for you.
1 PETER 5:6–7

Everybody has problems. I'm sure you have some things that worry you too. Some of them can feel so big that you're not sure you'll get through them. But God doesn't want you to try to handle your problems all by yourself. In fact, it's prideful to think that you can fix everything by yourself. So instead of trying to tough it out and handle things on your own, trust your problems to God. And you *can* trust Him because, as your heavenly Father, He loves you.

Father, I'm sorry that I haven't prayed about the things that are worrying me. I don't want to try to fix them on my own anymore. I trust You to help me. Today I need Your help with _____. In Jesus' name, amen.

Don't Forget to Say Thank You!

Go into His gates giving thanks and into His holy place with praise. Give thanks to Him. Honor His name. For the Lord is good. His loving-kindness lasts forever. And He is faithful to all people and to all their children-to-come.

PSALM 100:4–5

It's easy to remember to pray when things aren't going well, when you feel like you really need God's help with a big problem. But what about the days when life seems great? Do you remember to give thanks to your heavenly Father for all the amazing blessings He's poured into your life? He doesn't want to hear from you only on the hard days; He wants to have a relationship with you every day. So thank Him for the wins, for good friends, and for happy days too.

God, I'm sorry if I have forgotten to thank You for blessing me with good things. Today I want to thank You for _____. In Jesus' name, amen.

Pray for Understanding

*For the Lord gives wisdom. Much learning
and understanding come from His mouth.
He stores up perfect wisdom for those who
are right with Him. He is a safe-covering
to those who are right in their walk.*

PROVERBS 2:6–7

Some things in life are hard to understand—like advanced math and why bad things happen to people who are good. But what's even more incredible? You have a loving heavenly Father who isn't afraid of your questions. He's not stumped by even the hardest equations or problems in life because He is all-knowing and sees the whole world and all of time in one big picture. So if you need understanding, ask Him today. Read your Bible and pray for understanding.

*God, You created this whole world, from the
tiny cells in my body to our solar system. You
actually do know it all. Who better to help me
understand as I read my Bible and try to live my
life following Jesus. God, today I need Your help
understanding _____. In Jesus' name, amen.*

Share Jesus

*"For God so loved the world that He
gave His only Son. Whoever puts his
trust in God's Son will not be lost but
will have life that lasts forever."*

JOHN 3:16

We have an enemy in this world. Satan doesn't want
you to tell others about Jesus. And he wants to trick
the world into believing the lies that God doesn't exist
or care about people. But as a follower of Jesus, you
can fight against the enemy by praying for the people
around you who don't know about Jesus—and by sharing the good news with them.

*God, I have friends, neighbors, and family members
who don't know about Jesus. They don't know that You
love them with this big love or that Jesus died so their
sins could be forgiven. They don't know that eternal
life is waiting for them if they believe in You. Give
me boldness today to share the good news of Jesus
with them. Today I want to pray for _____
because they don't know You. In Jesus' name, amen.*

20

Ask God for Wisdom

If you do not have wisdom, ask God for it.
He is always ready to give it to you and
will never say you are wrong for asking.

JAMES 1:5

- -

What do you think of when you hear the word *wisdom*? Your grandpa and gray hair maybe? But wisdom isn't just for old people. Wisdom is just knowing what is right and doing it. And you can ask God for wisdom now, as a kid. When you know your parents' rules and follow them, you're showing wisdom. Being a wise kid can protect you from making bad decisions with painful consequences. The Bible also tells us that wisdom is worth more than anything you can buy (Proverbs 3:15) and that your wise choices as a kid will pay off when you're older (Proverbs 3:35).

Heavenly Father, help me make wise choices. I want to avoid lots of problems by being wise, and I want to share wisdom with my friends! In Jesus' name, amen.

Pray for Peace

*Be at peace with all men. Live a
holy life. No one will see the Lord
without having that kind of life.*
HEBREWS 12:14

- - - - - - - - - - - - - - - - - -

Some people can be really hard to get along with. Maybe
they're rude to you or they make fun of you. But God
wants you to live a holy life—no matter what the people
around you are doing. He wants you to have peace with
the people in your life. Treat others with kindness even
if they aren't very nice in return. And forgive people
when they mess up. Don't keep ugly feelings of bit-
terness and anger around. Pray for peace.

*Heavenly Father, help me be strong and have peace
with the people around me as much as I can. Help me
make wise choices and do the right thing so my life will
tell others that I follow Jesus. Today I need Your help to
have peace with _____. In Jesus' name, amen.*

Pray for Your Parents

"Honor your father and your mother, as the Lord your God has told you. So your life may be long and it may go well with you in the land the Lord your God gives you."

DEUTERONOMY 5:16

- -

It's important to pray for your parents. After all, they're the ones guiding you and teaching you how to live. I'm sure they would love knowing that you were asking God to give them a little help with the huge responsibility of being your mom and dad. You can also ask for His help in obeying and honoring them, because, let's face it, being obedient can be tough. But honoring your parents comes with a special blessing: things will go well with you. And who doesn't want their life to turn out well?

Heavenly Father, thank You for my parents. Please help them make wise decisions, and teach me how to do what's right and follow Your Word. Help me honor them and be obedient to them. Today I need Your help honoring them by _____. In Jesus' name, amen.

Pray for Your Enemies

"I say to you who hear Me, love those who work against you. Do good to those who hate you. Respect and give thanks for those who try to bring bad to you. Pray for those who make it very hard for you."
LUKE 6:27–28

- - - - - - - - - - - - - - - - - -

Do you have any enemies? You know, the bully at school, the kid who always teases you, or maybe even a friend who hurt you. The Bible tells us that we shouldn't wish terrible things would happen to them or even treat them as badly as they've treated us. Instead, Jesus says to forgive them. Your forgiveness doesn't make what they did okay. God still sees how they've hurt you. But forgiveness does leave you feeling clean in spite of the hurt.

Lord, sometimes it's very hard not to treat mean people with unkindness. But I want to please You, Jesus. I pray that You would help _____ to see that You love them too. Help me be kind and forgive them. In Jesus' name, amen.

Forgive Me, Father

If we tell Him our sins, He is faithful and we can depend on Him to forgive us of our sins. He will make our lives clean from all sin.

1 JOHN 1:9

- -

We all mess up sometimes. The Bible tells us that we were born sinners because we live in a fallen world. It's important to see when you do things that are wrong and then ask the person you've hurt for forgiveness. But don't stop there. When King David sinned, he realized that his biggest sin was against God. And he prayed for God to forgive him. The Bible says that if we ask for God's forgiveness, He's faithful to forgive us.

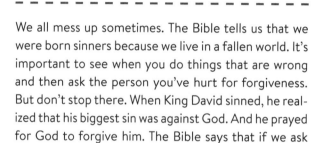

Heavenly Father, I messed up. I did something wrong, and I hurt people around me. But most of all, Father, I hurt You. Please forgive me for _____, and make me stronger so I don't make the same mistakes again. In Jesus' name, amen.

Courage, Dear Heart!

*"Be strong and have strength of heart! Do
not be afraid or lose faith. For the Lord
your God is with you anywhere you go."*

JOSHUA 1:9

Have you ever walked into a dark basement and felt fear slither down your spine at an unexpected noise? Or maybe you had to stand up in front of your whole class and give a report with shaking legs? You aren't the only child of God who has had to face fears. Joshua was about to take over as leader of the Israelites to lead them into the Promised Land (you know, the Promised Land that was filled with giants and fortress cities), and God gave him the encouraging words of Joshua 1:9 to boost his courage. Remember, the same God is with you too—everywhere you go.

*Heavenly Father, thank You for reminding me
that I can have courage in spite of my fears
because You are with me. Help me have courage
when I _____. In Jesus' name, amen.*

What Love Is

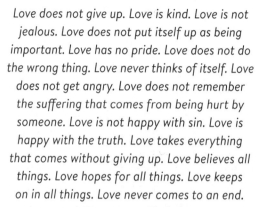

Love does not give up. Love is kind. Love is not jealous. Love does not put itself up as being important. Love has no pride. Love does not do the wrong thing. Love never thinks of itself. Love does not get angry. Love does not remember the suffering that comes from being hurt by someone. Love is not happy with sin. Love is happy with the truth. Love takes everything that comes without giving up. Love believes all things. Love hopes for all things. Love keeps on in all things. Love never comes to an end.

1 CORINTHIANS 13:4–8

- -

Today's world has a lot of different ideas about what love looks like. But don't be confused by things that people say. The Bible tells us what love looks like—and that is how God loves you too! Today, read through 1 Corinthians 13:4–8. Then finish this sentence: I could love better by being more _____and less _____.

Heavenly Father, thank You for loving me with a First Corinthians kind of love. Please help me be more _____. Amen.

27

Key to Contentment

*I know how to get along with little and how
to live when I have much. I have learned the
secret of being happy at all times. If I am full
of food and have all I need, I am happy. If I am
hungry and need more, I am happy. I can do all
things because Christ gives me the strength.*

PHILIPPIANS 4:12–13

- - - - - - - - - - - - - - - - - - - -

Contentment is a big word. It means being happy with
the things that you already have. The Bible tells us not
to be jealous of the stuff that other people have. If
you are struggling with wanting what you don't have,
remember that being thankful is the cure for jealousy.
Today, make a list of every good thing in your life, and
thank God for all of it. You'll start feeling so good about
your life. And remember that God makes you strong
when things are hard.

*Lord, today I want to thank You for _____.
Help me resist the temptation to want things. Give
me contentment and thankfulness for every good
thing You've given me. In Jesus' name, amen.*

Strong Joy

*"Do not be sad for the joy of
the Lord is your strength."*
NEHEMIAH 8:10

- - - - - - - - - - - - - - - - - - -

Some days it can be hard to find something to be happy about. Maybe nothing seems to be going your way or you've been disappointed. On these days, being joyful like the Bible says feels like a little too much to hope for. But having joy doesn't always mean skipping through your day singing. Your joy doesn't come from only good things happening to you; instead, it should flow out of your love for God and knowing that He cares for you and sent His Son to die on the cross so you could be His child. When you find joy in loving God, it will make you strong.

*Father, give me joy in knowing You. Even when things
aren't going the way I want them to, I know that You
still love me. And my future is already set—I'm going
to spend eternity with You. Thank You for Jesus
and His sacrifice for me. In Jesus' name, amen.*

Patience, Please

Rest in the Lord and be willing to wait for Him. Do not trouble yourself when all goes well with the one who carries out his sinful plans. Stop being angry. Turn away from fighting. Do not trouble yourself. It leads only to wrong-doing. For those who do wrong will be cut off. But those who wait for the Lord will be given the earth.

PSALM 37:7–9

Patience can be super hard when you're young. It seems like someone is always telling you to wait. But your parents have important reasons for asking you to wait for things—and God does too. God wants you to learn patience and wait for Him so He can do good things for you. When we're impatient and try to do things our way, things don't usually go so well. It may seem like people who do wrong things are getting ahead, but the Bible says that in the end they won't prosper.

Lord, please help me be patient and wait for the plans that You have for me. Amen.

Show Some Self-Control

*A man who cannot rule his own spirit is
like a city whose walls are broken down.*
PROVERBS 25:28

If you're into sports, you've probably heard the expression "Offense wins games. Defense wins championships." If you have no defense, anyone can score—and you lose. Well, the major protection of ancient cities was their walls. The Bible tells us that if you don't have self-control—whether it's with your temper, food, screen time, or doing stuff without thinking—then you are like a city with broken-down walls. You've got no protection from the enemy. Ask God to help you use self-control so you don't make foolish decisions that will cost you in the game of life.

*Heavenly Father, make me strong in self-control.
I don't want to live without protection against
the enemy. Help me do the right thing even when
I don't feel like it. Today I need Your help to have
self-control with _____. In Jesus' name, amen.*

Gentle Giant

*Live and work without pride. Be gentle
and kind. Do not be hard on others.
Let love keep you from doing that.*

EPHESIANS 4:2

- - - - - - - - - - - - - - - - - -

The world says that it's okay to be competitive and pushy
to get what we want. "Always look out for number one."
"Do what's best for you." Those are the messages of
our time. Gentleness isn't really given much credit. In
a world of bullies, we learn to fight. And people think if
you're gentle, you're weak. But Jesus said to be gentle
because He is gentle. Sometimes love means giving
something up for another person or speaking calm,
kind words when you're angry. Doing that takes a giant
love for Jesus.

*God, sometimes I want to win. I want the things
that I'd like to have. And sometimes I might
step on other people's feelings or needs to get
my own way. Help me be gentler when dealing
with _____. In Jesus' name, amen.*

Do Good Work

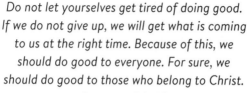

Do not let yourselves get tired of doing good.
If we do not give up, we will get what is coming
to us at the right time. Because of this, we
should do good to everyone. For sure, we
should do good to those who belong to Christ.
GALATIANS 6:9–10

- - - - - - - - - - - - - - - - -

Did you know that God has a job for you? He does! He's
got plans for all the good He'd like to do in this world
through none other than *you*. Sometimes it seems like
no one notices when you're good. But God sees every
time you choose to be good to someone else. Maybe
you helped your mom clean up the dishes when you'd
rather watch TV. You're building up heavenly rewards
by spreading goodness.

Father, I need Your help to be good in a world where
doing the wrong thing seems to be getting people
what they want. I know that You see the good I'm
doing. Show me the people around me who I can
help with a good deed. In Jesus' name, amen.

Disappointed

We know that God makes all things work
together for the good of those who love Him
and are chosen to be a part of His plan.

ROMANS 8:28

- - - - - - - - - - - - - - - - - - - -

You're so upset! You had plans to go spend time with your friends this weekend, but now you're stuck at home sick. We all get disappointed sometimes. And it can be really easy to have a big fit when things don't go our way. But one thing that might brighten your gloomy thoughts is to remember that God is in control. He can take even the not-so-nice things that happen and use them for something good. Maybe your dad took the day off, and the two of you laughed and watched funny movies all day. When you love God and follow His ways, He can use the bad stuff for good.

Lord, help me with my disappointment when things
don't go my way. I want to use self-control when
my plans change. Help me trust in You and look
for how You are using this for good. Amen.

Prayer Power

*Tell your sins to each other. And pray
for each other so you may be healed.
The prayer from the heart of a man
right with God has much power.*

JAMES 5:16

- -

Have you ever wondered why the Bible says we should pray? After all, if God knows everything, why does He need us to tell Him or even ask for things? The Bible tells us that God listens to our prayers. He hears every word. Your prayers aren't to help Him out. They're meant to help you out. God wants you to learn to trust Him and see that He hears and answers your prayers. He wants a relationship with you because He thinks you're pretty special. And the only way you can get to know Him is to read His Word and talk to Him—and the more you talk to Him and learn His ways, the more you'll grow and change.

*Father, my prayers mean something. They can
change me and the world around me. Thank You for
listening to me. Thank You for loving me. Amen.*

Asking for a Friend

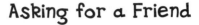

You do not get things because you do not ask for them. Or if you do ask, you do not receive because your reasons for asking are wrong. You want these things only to please yourselves.

JAMES 4:2–3

- -

Have you ever asked for something you really wanted, but you didn't get it? Sometimes we're a little selfish when we pray. You might ask that your parents would buy you that new video game or new shoes. Jesus taught that we should not be selfish. And that includes our prayers. Now, that doesn't mean you can't ask God to bless you with things that you want. But God also wants you to grow to be more like Jesus—and that means thinking about what others need and what God wants. Try it today. Pray for the good of another person.

God, I'm sorry that sometimes I'm all wrapped up in myself. Open my eyes and help me see that there are people around me who need Your help. Today I ask that You would help _____. In Jesus' name, amen.

Integrity

"Do what is right and good in the eyes of the Lord. Then it will be well with you."

DEUTERONOMY 6:18

- -

What does it mean to have integrity? Integrity means doing what God says is right—all the time, even when no one is looking. Integrity is important if you want people to trust you. If you always choose to do right, others will notice. And have you noticed a trend about doing what God says is right? Yep, there's a blessing in it for you! The Bible says that it will be well with you, and who doesn't want things to go well? God loves you and doesn't want to see you go down a bumpy and painful road of foolish decisions. That's why He teaches you to live with integrity.

Heavenly Father, I want to do the right thing. Help me live with integrity, even when no one else is looking, because I know that You see everything I do, and You even see the motives of my heart. Today help me have integrity with _____ . In Jesus' name, amen.

Hmm. . .What to Pray

Jesus said to them, "When you pray, say, 'Our Father in heaven, Your name is holy. May Your holy nation come. What You want done, may it be done on earth as it is in heaven. Give us the bread we need everyday. Forgive us our sins, as we forgive those who sin against us. Do not let us be tempted.' "

Luke 11:2–4

- - - - - - - - - - - - - - - - - - - -

You can pray about anything. But here are a few things that God thinks are important to pray about:

1. **The things you need.**
2. **The things other people need.**
3. **That what God wants will be done.**
4. **Praise Him for how awesome He is!**

Heavenly Father, today I need _____. And I know someone who needs _____. Help me do what You want today, God, instead of what I want. And thanks for being so great! Amen.

He Can Help!

*I cried to the Lord in my trouble, and He
answered me and put me in a good place.*
PSALM 118:5

- -

When you're having problems in life or are worried,
the best place to be is in prayer with God. He's the
One who created you. And you need Him. He gives
you life, and the Bible says that "Christ was before all
things. All things are held together by Him" (Colossians
1:17). I guess that's God's way of saying that He's got
this! He has all the wisdom, all the power, and all the
knowledge needed to help you with your troubles.
He's really the only one who can help you. And He
doesn't mind at all when you bring your problems to
Him. Because He loves you.

*Heavenly Father, thank You that You're willing and
able to help me when I need it. Today I really need
help with _____ . In Jesus' name, amen.*

Off Limits

Let us go with complete trust to the throne of God. We will receive His loving-kindness and have His loving-favor to help us whenever we need it.
HEBREWS 4:16

- - - - - - - - - - - - - - - - -

Does God mind if you tell Him everything? Of course, you can pray about anything that is bothering you. You shouldn't pray for things that would be sinful or accuse God of doing bad things, because He is completely good. The Bible says that there's no bad in Him at all. He can't sin. But He wants to hear about the things that matter to you. And God can use your prayers to change you to be more like Jesus. If you're praying for something that's wrong, God will show you and help you change. You'll get closer to God the more you pray.

Heavenly Father, show me if something I've been asking You for isn't right or isn't part of how You want me to live. I know that I can tell You everything. In Jesus' name, amen.

Never Too Small

Give all your worries to Him
because He cares for you.
1 PETER 5:7

- -

You might wonder if God pays more attention to prayers about big, important things and if He has time for you too. Remember that God doesn't have the same limits that we humans do. Not only does He have all the power in the universe, but He can be everywhere at one time and hear every prayer that is prayed to Him. He can see the past and the future, and He doesn't have a beginning or an end. Your prayers are not too small for God's attention. In the Bible, Hannah prayed for a child, and Solomon asked God for wisdom. These people told God about their cares and what was important to them. So what are you thinking or worried about? Tell God about it today.

Heavenly Father, I'm so glad that my life matters to You. You care about how I'm doing. Today I need to talk to You about _____ . In Jesus' name, amen.

How Much Prayer Is Enough?

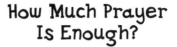

Never stop praying.
1 Thessalonians 5:17

Try not to think of prayer as just another thing to get done. Prayer shouldn't be a chore. Make a habit of praying and talking to God all the time. Why? Because He loves you and because He's on your side and promises to help you. Prayer is a chance to have a better relationship with the good and awesome God who created you and sent Jesus to save you. Talk to God because you love Him and not just to cross things off your to-do list. Lots of people like to think back on their day and pray about it at bedtime. But it's also great to have chats with God all day long—and at night you can thank Him for His help and tell Him how great He is.

Heavenly Father, I look forward to talking with You because I know that You love me and are always ready to hear what I'm thinking about. In Jesus' name, amen.

Idol Talk

They did know God, but they did not honor Him as God. They were not thankful to Him and thought only of foolish things. Their foolish minds became dark. They said that they were wise, but they showed how foolish they were. They gave honor to false gods that looked like people who can die and to birds and animals and snakes. This honor belongs to God Who can never die.

ROMANS 1:21–23

- -

Have you ever wished on a star or carried around a lucky rabbit's foot? These things don't actually have any power to help you, but God does. Some people choose not to believe in the living God who created everything, and they worship an idol. But unlike our God, who is alive and the powerful Creator of everything in this world, those idols are just things. They can't hear you or change your life. Trust God today, and see that He really does have the power to answer prayers.

Heavenly Father, I trust in You alone. I trust that You hear my prayers and answer. Today I want to talk to You about _____. Amen.

Good Friends

*Do not let anyone fool you. Bad people can
make those who want to live good become bad.
Keep your minds awake! Stop sinning. Some do
not know God at all. I say this to your shame.*
1 CORINTHIANS 15:33–34

- - - - - - - - - - - - - - - - -

Have you ever seen those funny pictures of people who
look like their pets? Sometimes we also start acting like
the people we hang out with. That's why God tells us to
be wise about the friends we choose. It's probably not
news to you that your friends can influence what you
think and do. When people are making wrong choices
and doing things that are not pleasing to God, the Bible says you shouldn't spend time with them because
they'll lead you away from God. Pray and ask God to
put friends in your life who also love Jesus and want to
do the right thing. This way you can encourage each
other to keep following Jesus.

*Heavenly Father, send me good friends who love
You. And I'm really thankful for _____,
who is such a great friend already. Amen.*

Resist!

"Watch and pray so that you will not be tempted. Man's spirit is willing, but the body does not have the power to do it."

MATTHEW 26:41

Sometimes things that we know are wrong can look pretty good. But remember that God has better plans for you when you do what He says is right. The Bible says doing wrong will always catch up with you in the end because you can't hide anything from God. So don't forget to pray that God will help you resist temptation. And don't forget your armor—the helmet of salvation, the breastplate of righteousness, the shield of faith, the sword of the Spirit, the belt of truth, and the Gospel shoes of peace. Open your Bible and read Ephesians 6:10–18 so you too can stand strong against the enemy.

Heavenly Father, help me stand strong when I am tempted. I want to choose right. Help me use the Bible verses I've memorized to fight against Satan. In Jesus' name, amen.

Surprising Answers

Then Moses put out his hand over the sea.
And the Lord moved the sea all night
by a strong east wind. So the waters
were divided. And the people of Israel
went through the sea on dry land.

EXODUS 14:21–22

- - - - - - - - - - - - - - - - - - -

Have you ever had a problem that you couldn't solve? It can be discouraging when you can't see a way out of your troubles. Have faith! God is much bigger and more powerful than you are. He can come up with solutions that you never even thought to ask for. Trust Him today. The Israelites got really upset with Moses when they escaped slavery in Egypt. The pharaoh's army came chasing after them, and they were backed up against the Red Sea. They thought they were going to die. But God did something unexpected. He opened the sea in front of them—and they walked through! He can do the same for you!

Lord, I know You have the wisdom and the power
to solve my problems. Show me the way
that I should go. In Jesus' name, amen.

Good Enough

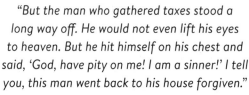

"But the man who gathered taxes stood a long way off. He would not even lift his eyes to heaven. But he hit himself on his chest and said, 'God, have pity on me! I am a sinner!' I tell you, this man went back to his house forgiven."
LUKE 18:13–14

Have you ever messed up and felt ashamed of your behavior—like maybe you shouldn't talk to God about your sin because He might be upset with you? Don't fall for the enemy's lie that God doesn't want to talk to you when you make a mistake. God sees your heart. And He can tell when you're sorry for what you've done. When we mess up, we need God more than ever. You should pray and admit that what you did was wrong and ask Him to forgive you. God wants to help you change and do better.

Heavenly Father, I messed up. Please forgive me for _____. Help me resist temptation in the future. I really want to do what is pleasing to You. Amen.

Start a Conversation with God

"Until now you have not asked for anything in My name. Ask and you will receive. Then your joy will be full."
JOHN 16:24

- -

We pray so we can get to know God better (He's pretty amazing). We also pray so we can grow closer to Him. Praying is like a long conversation. Think of your best friend and all the talks you've had together about tons of things—you know each other pretty well after all those chats. When you decide to follow Jesus, God starts to change the way you think and act so you'll be more like Jesus. God wants to be your friend and help you. He also wants to use you in His plans. Prayer lets God show you what to do and lets you tell God you want to do things His way instead of yours.

Heavenly Father, forgive me for the wrong things I've done today and for any selfish things I've done. I want to do Your will today instead of mine. In Jesus' name, amen.

Say Amen!

Honor and thanks be to the Lord, the God of Israel, forever and ever. Let all the people say, "Let it be so!" Praise the Lord!

PSALM 106:48

- -

So why exactly do we say "amen" at the end of our prayers? Maybe you've said it so many times you've never thought to ask why. *Amen* means "so be it" or "it is true." So when you say "amen" at the end of your prayer, you're asking God to please let things be as you've prayed. You believe that God listened to your prayer, and you trust Him to answer. It's also a way to show your agreement with others. So if someone else is praying out loud and you say "amen," it's your way of saying that you are standing with that person in prayer.

Heavenly Father, I trust You to hear and answer my prayers. And I want to help other Christians in their prayers too. Today I want to talk to You about _____. In Jesus' name, amen.

Because He Said So

Dear friends, you must become strong in your most holy faith. Let the Holy Spirit lead you as you pray. Keep yourselves in the love of God. Wait for life that lasts forever through the loving-kindness of our Lord Jesus Christ.

JUDE 20–21

Why is it so good to pray? The first and most important reason is because God tells us to do it. I know you probably get tired of hearing your parents say things like "because I said so," but when God says that something is good for you, you can totally trust Him because He is completely good and always wants what's best for you. Prayer also helps you get closer to God. It makes your relationship with Him deeper. It would be hard to get closer to your friends if you never talked to them. And God wants to be your friend too.

Heavenly Father, I trust that You're a good God who wants what's best for me. Today I want to tell You about _____. Amen.

A Pleasing Heart

He walked away from them about as far as a stone can be thrown. There He got down with His face on the ground and prayed. He said, "Father, if it can be done, take away what must happen to Me. Even so, not what I want, but what You want."
Luke 22:41–42

Maybe you kneel down to pray, or maybe you talk to God while you're lying in bed. Either way, He's still listening. The Bible talks about people who prayed in lots of different ways. Some of them raised their hands, some laid on the ground, and some knelt. You can bow your head and close your eyes, or you can stand up. Kneeling is a way to show respect to your heavenly Father—it can show that you're humble and ready to do things God's way. And this is just the kind of attitude God loves to see during your prayers.

Heavenly Father, I love You and know that You're listening. Give me an attitude that is pleasing to You when I pray. Amen.

Pray for Leaders

*When those who are right with God rule,
the people are glad, but when a sinful
man rules, the people have sorrow.*

PROVERBS 29:2

- - - - - - - - - - - - - - - - - -

If you're looking for some important people to add to
your prayer list today, remember to pray for the people
who are in charge of leading your country, your state,
and your community. You can even include your teachers, Sunday school teachers, and pastor. It's important
to pray that the people who run our government will
make wise choices, because what they do affects the
way we live. It's also important to pray that they will
come to know Jesus if they don't. That way they can
lead us in a way that pleases God.

*Heavenly Father, I pray for our president, senators,
congresspeople, governors, and mayors. I pray that You
will give them wisdom in the choices they make. And
I pray that You will bring someone into their lives to
tell them about Jesus if they don't know Him. I'd also
like to pray for _____. In Jesus' name, amen.*

Grace!

Honor and thanks be to the Lord, the God of Israel, forever and ever. Let all the people say, "Let it be so!" Praise the Lord!
PSALM 106:48

- - - - - - - - - - - - - - - - - - -

Has anyone ever asked you to say grace before dinner? The word *grace*, when we're talking about praying before a meal, means "thanksgiving." So it makes sense to call the dinner prayer "grace" because you're thanking God for the food He has given you and asking His blessing over your meal. Being thankful is important because God created everything, including the food that keeps us alive and well. Being grateful before a meal tells God that you know you need Him and that He provides everything you need.

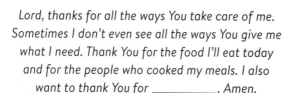

Lord, thanks for all the ways You take care of me. Sometimes I don't even see all the ways You give me what I need. Thank You for the food I'll eat today and for the people who cooked my meals. I also want to thank You for _____. Amen.

A Real Need

He told the people to sit down on the grass.
Then He took the five loaves of bread and two
fish. He looked up to heaven and gave thanks.
He broke the loaves in pieces and gave them
to His followers. The followers gave them to
the people. They all ate and were filled.
MATTHEW 14:19–20

One day a huge crowd was following Jesus and listening to Him teach. They were all getting hungry but didn't have any food. Jesus took one little boy's lunch of bread and fish and fed over five thousand people. He can take care of you too. God promises to provide the things that we need. This doesn't mean that God will give you everything you ask Him for—He's not a vending machine. But you can trust Him to take care of you because God always keeps His promises.

Lord, I know that sometimes I want things that I can
live without. Some of them may end up not being
so good for me anyway. But today I really need
_____. Please help me. In Jesus' name, amen.

Prayer Warrior

*I thank God for you. I pray for you night
and day. I am working for God the
way my early fathers worked. My
heart says I am free from sin.*
2 TIMOTHY 1:3

- - - - - - - - - - - - - - - - - - - -

Have your parents ever labeled someone in your family
or church a "prayer warrior"? What exactly does this
mean? Usually this means they pray all the time. They
pray for other people and God's work in the world
every day. We all should develop the habit of praying
often, but some people feel that God has given them
the special job of spending a lot of time praying for the
work of building His kingdom—it's part of His special
purpose for them. Make a list of ways you can pray
for God's kingdom, like praying for missionaries, your
pastor, or the leaders of your country. And you can be
a prayer warrior too!

*Heavenly Father, today I want to pray for
_____ and the special work that they do
to build Your kingdom. In Jesus' name, amen.*

55

First Things First

*Christy was before all things. All
things are held together by Him.*

COLOSSIANS 1:17

- - - - - - - - - - - - - - - -

Praise the Lord every day. He's here for you. He loves
you. He's got everything under control. What's not to
praise? Don't wait until everything is unraveling and
you feel like God is your last hope before you pray to
Him about your problems. Remember Him—and His
amazing love for you—every day. Go to Him first instead
of last. You can talk to Him about everything, your big
problems and small ones. You don't have to rely only on
yourself in life. God's on your side. And praying about
your struggles can help prevent them from becoming
really big problems too.

*Heavenly Father, I don't want to forget about
You. Instead I want to talk to You first when
I've got problems. Today I want to talk to You
about _____. In Jesus' name, amen.*

Was That Long Enough?

This is why I have never stopped praying for you since I heard about you. I ask God that you may know what He wants you to do.

<small>COLOSSIANS 1:9</small>

- - - - - - - - - - - - - - - - - - -

Sometimes the prayers you hear in church can be pretty long. You might wonder if God gets tired listening to long prayers or if it's better to pray for a really long time. But don't forget that God listens to the prayers of kids, whether they are short or long, just as much as He listens to the many prayer requests during church. Your pastor might pray long prayers because he has a lot to pray about—many people ask for prayer about lots of different things. While you're listening, remember to pray along silently too.

Lord, I know You hear all my prayers, even the short ones. Give me a heart that cares about what other people need so I can pray for them too. Today I want to pray for _____. Amen.

Get Well Soon!

*Is anyone among you sick? He should send
for the church leaders and they should pray
for him. They should pour oil on him in the
name of the Lord. The prayer given in faith
will heal the sick man, and the Lord will raise
him up. If he has sinned, he will be forgiven.*

JAMES 5:14–15

- - - - - - - - - - - - - - - - - - -

Should you pray for someone who is sick to get better?
And what if they don't get better? Remember that
God has more wisdom than we do, and He can see
every person everywhere, and He knows everyone's
concerns. Yes, He is powerful enough to heal the sick,
and sometimes when you pray for the sick, miracles
happen. You can also pray that God will give the doc-
tors wisdom in how to treat what's wrong. But sometimes God doesn't make people better. Sometimes
God teaches them how to be joyful and trust Him in
the midst of hard things like illness or disability.

*Heavenly Father, _____ is sick. I pray that
You would heal them, but I trust Your answer. Amen.*

A Pick-Me-Up

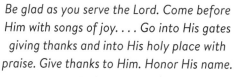

Be glad as you serve the Lord. Come before Him with songs of joy. . . . Go into His gates giving thanks and into His holy place with praise. Give thanks to Him. Honor His name.
PSALM 100:2, 4

When everything starts feeling like it's stacked against you, remember to thank God for all the great things in your life. You really do have a great life! For one thing, you're alive! You get to live this amazing day with all its potential that God has planned for you. Look at your life and see how many good things you can list. Are you healthy? Do you live in a warm house, have a loving family, get to go to school? Do you play any sports you love? Breathe in the air that keeps you alive, and thank God that you're here today!

Heavenly Father, thank You that I can live for You and do good for others. I might have some hard times, but I know You love me and will never leave me. Amen.

Keep Talking

"I say to you, ask, and what you ask for will be given to you. Look, and what you are looking for you will find. Knock, and the door you are knocking on will be opened to you."

Luke 11:9

- - - - - - - - - - - - - - - - -

Have you ever had a good friend who moved away? You probably didn't talk as much anymore, did you? And pretty soon you were like strangers. This is what happens when we don't pray. We miss out on getting to know God more. We also lose out on His help. When we talk to God a lot, we often see the ways that He changes us or the things around us. And He teaches us the things that are important to Him. Don't cut yourself off from God and the close relationship He wants to have with you. Talk to Him every day so you don't grow apart.

Heavenly Father, I don't want to miss out on knowing You or getting the help I need. Help me find a good time every day to chat with You. Today I want to tell You about _____. Amen.

He's King

Do not hurry to speak or be in a hurry as you think what to tell God. For God is in heaven and you are on the earth. So let your words be few.
ECCLESIASTES 5:1–2

- - - - - - - - - - - - - - - - - - - -

You might wonder if it's okay to use memorized prayers when you're talking to God. Learning to pray using something like the Lord's Prayer is a good thing. It teaches you about what's important to God. But sometimes we speed through memorized words without really stopping to think about what we're saying to God. God wants you to be thoughtful about your words when you pray and to remember who He is—the King of everything! Whether you're praying a memorized prayer or using your own words, always make sure you're focused and being real with God.

Heavenly Father, I want to focus on You when I'm praying and not rush through or get distracted. Today I want to ask for Your help with _____. Amen.

Prayer Interrupted

*Then He went away by
Himself to pray in a desert.*
LUKE 5:16

- - - - - - - - - - - - - - - -

Interruptions happen. Sometimes they're fun, like when you don't really want to clean your room and your best friend calls. Or they can be unpleasant, like when your mom says during your favorite video game that it's time to do your homework. Sometimes our prayers get interrupted too. Life happens and something comes up. But prayer is just like talking to your best friend—you can pick up right where you left off the next time. If you find that every time you try to pray you get interrupted by something, you could try what Jesus did. He found a quiet space, all by Himself, with no distractions so He could talk to His Father.

*Lord, today I'm going to find a place where I can
be alone for a bit with You. I have some important
things to talk to You about, like _____.
Thanks for always being there to help me. Amen.*

Getting to Know Him

The Lord hates the gifts of the sinful,
but the prayer of the faithful is His joy.
PROVERBS 15:8

- - - - - - - - - - - - - - - - - -

Your prayers bring a smile to God's face. He's glad to hear from you. God is delighted to spend time with you, just like a dad who loves to spend time with his children. You can get to know your heavenly Father, not just know *about* Him, by spending time with Him. Who is your favorite movie star or sports hero? I bet you'd recognize their picture anywhere. But you don't actually know them like you know your dad—his favorite food and hobby, whether he's funny. . .So how can you know God like this? Well, you have a relationship with your father because you spend time with him. You can spend time with your heavenly Father as well, by reading your Bible, praying, and spending time worshipping.

Lord, I want to get to know You better. I want
to know what You're like and what makes You
smile and what makes You sad. Today I want
to talk to You about _____. Amen.

63

Plan Daily Prayer

Be full of joy all the time. Never stop praying.
In everything give thanks. This is what God
wants you to do because of Christ Jesus.
1 THESSALONIANS 5:16–18

- - - - - - - - - - - - - - - - - - -

What are some times in your day when you could pray?
The Bible says to pray all the time and that God loves
chatting with you anytime, just like your mom loves it
when you come through the kitchen but still stop to say
hi and give her an update on your day. But your mom
also loves to have some special time when you can really
talk, and so does God. Remember that you can pray out
loud or quietly to yourself. And be sure to add some
quiet time to your talks so He can speak to you too.

Father, show me times in my day that I could set aside
for special talks, just me and You. I really want to hear
what You have to tell me. And I want to share all the
details of my day with You. In Jesus' name, amen.

Get Creative Part 1

"Look to the Lord and ask for His strength. Look to Him all the time."
1 Chronicles 16:11

- - - - - - - - - - - - - - - - - - -

Have you ever wondered why people make such a big deal about prayer? It's because prayer isn't boring like some people might try to convince you. It's how you build a relationship with God. You can make your prayer times fun by trying different things:

Practice Praise. Worship God for how amazing He is—and you get to decide how. Paint Him a picture, sing Him a song. Be creative!

Say Thank You. You're surrounded by blessings. What can you thank Him for today? Start a thankfulness journal, and write down a few things every day.

God, You're so amazing! I'm wowed by Your love for me. Today I praise You for _____. And, God, I have so much to be thankful for today. Thank You for _____. In Jesus' name, amen.

Get Creative Part 2

You must pray at all times as the Holy Spirit leads you to pray. Pray for the things that are needed. You must watch and keep on praying. Remember to pray for all Christians.

EPHESIANS 6:18

- - - - - - - - - - - - - - - - - -

Remember that God loves you and wants to get to know you. And He wants you to know Him. You can make this happen by talking to God about how you feel in lots of different ways. Make sure your prayers don't end up sounding like "me, me, me."

Think of Others. Don't forget to pray for other people—your brothers and sisters, mom, dad, grandma, grandpa, friends, and neighbors. If you're thinking about them, pray for God to help them too.

You Too. Make a list of the things you need God's help with, and ask Him. He loves you and wants to help.

Heavenly Father, bring to my mind the people that You want me to pray for today. _____ really needs Your help. And Father, I ask that You would help me with _____. In Jesus' name, amen.

Get Creative Part 3

If we tell Him our sins, He is faithful and we
can depend on Him to forgive us of our sins.
1 JOHN 1:9

- - - - - - - - - - - - - - - - - - - -

It's important to remember to pray about the things you need and also to pray for other people and praise God, but there's something that sometimes gets overlooked in our prayers. Maybe because admitting that you did something wrong can be hard. But God loves you very much. And the Bible promises that if we admit our sins, repent (which means to change your mind and choose to do right), and ask His forgiveness, He'll forgive you—every time.

Say You're Sorry. We all mess up sometimes. What are the sins you need to confess and ask God to forgive you for? God will always forgive you. And telling Him you're sorry helps you remember how much you need Him.

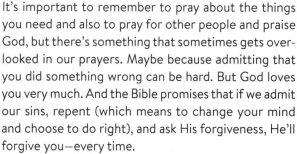

Heavenly Father, I did something wrong, and I
sinned against You. I'm so sorry for _____.
I'm choosing to turn around and follow You.
Please forgive me. In Jesus' name, amen.

God Is Good

*Trust in the Lord with all your heart, and
do not trust in your own understanding.
Agree with Him in all your ways, and
He will make your paths straight.*

PROVERBS 3:5–6

- - - - - - - - - - - - - - - - - -

Can you think of some big moments in your life—things
you'll remember forever? Meeting your baby sister,
finding a best friend, winning an award. . . Or maybe
the time you remember the most is when God helped
you when you were having a really hard time. Write
down all these life-changing moments, and read them
often to remind yourself that God is good and you can
trust Him.

*Heavenly Father, thank You for all the good
and amazing things You've done for me—the
times You've helped me through pain and fears,
and the times You've blessed me with success
and friends and family who love me. Some of
my favorite moments in life are _____.
Thank You for these. In Jesus' name, amen.*

Always Thankful

*You must keep praying. Keep
watching! Be thankful always.*
COLOSSIANS 4:2

Take a moment to think about your life. What things are you grateful for today? Maybe you have a really great mom or dad. Or your teacher helps you love learning, or you're awesome at sports. Maybe you're an artist, or your best friend always understands you. Whether it's a new bike or a pet that you adore, all these great things came from a good God who loves you. Try grabbing a piece of paper and making a list of ten things that you're thankful God has put in your life. Sometimes it's easy to get distracted by the negative things and miss the many good things you have.

*Heavenly Father, thank You so much for _____.
I don't want to miss all the ways You are there for
me every day. Help me recognize all the blessings
You've planted in my life. In Jesus' name, amen.*

Sing Loud

Come, let us sing with joy to the Lord. Let us sing loud with joy to the rock Who saves us. Let us come before Him giving thanks. Let us make a sound of joy to Him with songs. For the Lord is a great God, and a great King above all gods.

PSALM 95:1–3

– – – – – – – – – – – – – – – – – – –

There are all sorts of reasons to praise God—family, good friends, wonderful weather, or yummy food and clean water. But one of the best of God's gifts to us is Jesus. God loves you so much that He sent His own Son to die for you so you could have a never-ending future with Him. From the big things to the small ones, God is overjoyed to hear your praise.

Father, You've given so much, from beautiful butterflies to another day of life. And most of all, You gave me Jesus. Not only did He die for me, but He's also my friend. You have done amazing things. No one else could ever measure up to You. In Jesus' name, amen.

Do the Right Thing

*If you know what is right to do
but you do not do it, you sin.*
JAMES 4:17

- -

God has put you here—at this time in history, in your neighborhood, and in your specific family—for a purpose. But we can miss out on great things God has in store for us by ignoring His Word and doing whatever feels comfortable to us. The Bible says that if you know what the right thing to do is and don't do it, then you sin. Don't miss out on the greatness of doing good for God's kingdom. Go out there and do right!

God, I don't want to miss out on Your blessings because I'm choosing to do the wrong thing or just doing whatever feels good to me without obeying Your Word. I don't want to sin against You, heavenly Father. Make me bold and strong to do what's right. In Jesus' name, amen.

Tell Him Everything

*Trust in the Lord with all your heart, and
do not trust in your own understanding.
Agree with Him in all your ways, and
He will make your paths straight.*

PROVERBS 3:5–6

- - - - - - - - - - - - - - - - - - - -

No matter what you're going through in life, pray about
it. Just like your best friend wants to hear everything,
God wants you to talk to Him too. He loves you so much,
and He has all the answers to any problems or bumps
in your road. He understands both your happiness and
your pains. And He gives the best advice. He will help
you make wise choices in your life that will take you in
the right direction. Talk to Him today, and trust Him
to help you.

*Heavenly Father, the best thing happening in my
life right now is _____. I'm so glad I can
share it with You and thank You for the goodness
in my life. The hardest thing I'm struggling with
right now is _____. I could really use Your
help and guidance to make a good decision
about this. In Jesus' name, amen.*

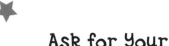

Ask for Your Father's Advice

My help comes from the Lord,
Who made heaven and earth.
PSALM 121:2

God wants you to be a wise person who makes wise choices. There's a difference between being smart and being wise. Wisdom comes only from God. You can grow in wisdom by studying God's Word and learning what God says is the right way to live. You can also pray for God to give you wisdom to make the best decisions with your life. Ask God what He thinks, and make sure you are reading your Bible. Leave some quiet space in your prayer time too for God to share His wisdom with you.

Heavenly Father, thank You for wanting to share
Your wisdom with me. It's really amazing that
You—the powerful God who made everything—
want to share Your wisdom with me. You really
care about the choices I make! Today I need to ask
for Your advice about _____. Please help
me make a wise choice. In Jesus' name, amen.

Put God First

*"First of all, look for the holy nation of
God. Be right with Him. All these other
things will be given to you also."*
<small>MATTHEW 6:33</small>

- - - - - - - - - - - - - - - - -

What does it look like to put God first? It means that
building your relationship with God becomes the most
important thing in your life. It means that talking to
Him all the time and reading your Bible become top
priorities in your day. And it means that trying to live
God's way becomes your number one goal. You put Him
above your favorite TV show or your soccer practice or
even spending time with your friends. Your love for Him
means that He comes first, no matter what.

*Heavenly Father, I love You so much for the
way that You take care of me and are always
there for me. I love You because You sent Jesus
to save me. Show me how I can put You first in
every part of my life. In Jesus' name, amen.*

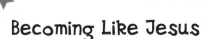

Becoming Like Jesus

"I have done this to show you what should be done. You should do as I have done to you."
JOHN 13:15

Your parents are pretty smart when they tell you to be careful about the friends you choose to hang out with. They know that it's important to choose close friends who also want to do what God says is right. Even more important, the more you spend time with God, the more you'll act like Him! You'll start making wise choices because you know that it will please your heavenly Father. When you memorize Bible verses and pray often, God will help you to not do things like get annoyed with your little sister. And the people around you will notice that you're becoming more like Jesus.

Heavenly Father, I'm so thankful that I'm part of Your family. I want to spend so much time with You that I look just like Jesus with everything I say and do. Today I could really use Your help with _____. In Jesus' name, amen.

Do Good!

Do not let yourselves get tired of doing good. If we do not give up, we will get what is coming to us at the right time.

Galatians 6:9

- -

Is it really worth it to do the right thing? After all, no one seems to notice when you help with a smile or turn in your homework on time. And it seems like the mean and selfish kids have more stuff than you do. But don't give up! God sees every single kind word and unselfish act. And He will reward you in His time. Even if it seems like doing wrong will get you ahead in this world, the Bible says that there's a terrible end for those who keep doing wrong. So keep on working for God. . .even when you feel like no one cares. God does!

Heavenly Father, I know You'll reward me for doing good. Today I need help choosing to do right by _____. In Jesus' name, amen.

Of Great Worth

*"I tell you, it is the same way among the angels
of God. If one sinner is sorry for his sins and
turns from them, the angels are very happy."*
LUKE 15:10

Have you ever misplaced your money? Jesus told a story
about a woman who lost a coin. She swept her whole
house until she found her lost coin. I bet you looked
really hard for your lost money too! Why? Because
money is valuable. Jesus told this parable because in
God's eyes, you are that coin. You're special to Him
and worth a lot in His eyes. To repent means to turn
away from your sins and ask God for forgiveness—it's
choosing to live life His way. The angels celebrate every
person who comes to know Jesus as their Savior. That
includes you. If you haven't, tell God you want to turn
away from doing wrong, and trust Jesus as your Savior.

*God, thank You for Jesus. Thank You that I'm
precious to You. I need to turn away from doing
_____ and ask for Your forgiveness. Amen.*

Send Help!

I pray that because of the riches of His shining-greatness, He will make you strong with power in your hearts through the Holy Spirit.

EPHESIANS 3:16

- - - - - - - - - - - - - - - - - - -

God wants His children to have virtue—that means "to be good." He wants you to make wise choices, treat people with kindness and love, and serve others . . .even when it's hard. Doing the right thing all the time might sound impossible, but God will help you! In fact, He has given you a secret weapon. When you follow Jesus, the Holy Spirit comes to live in your heart. The Holy Spirit is your Helper who makes you strong so you can choose to do the right thing. Try it today! Pray and ask the Holy Spirit to make you strong and give you the power to choose good.

Lord, I want to do what You say is right, but I'm struggling right now. Please make me strong with the power of Your Holy Spirit so I can do the right thing. In Jesus' name, amen.

No Drama

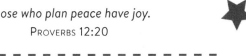

Those who plan peace have joy.
PROVERBS 12:20

- -

Exciting things can be great. Who doesn't love a birthday party or a ball game? But beware of people who think it's fun to stir up trouble. Do you have any friends who love to stir up drama? Maybe they spread rumors or make things that happen sound worse than they are just to get everyone upset. Drama is exhausting, and the Bible tells us to work toward peace. Instead of the wrong kind of joy found in causing trouble, God wants you to have true joy in peace—like the easy good times you have when you're getting along. The next time you're tempted to stir up a little strife, ask yourself, "Am I working for peace with my friends, siblings, and parents? Or am I stirring up trouble?" Be a peacemaker. The reward is joy!

Heavenly Father, I'm sorry for the times I've caused trouble. I want the real joy that I'll have from getting along. Please help me work for peace. In Jesus' name, amen.

Time for What's Important

*They said to Him, "We have only
five loaves of bread and two fish."
Jesus said, "Bring them to Me."*
MATTHEW 14:17–18

- -

We're late. Hurry up. Rush, rush, rush. No time! Do any of these statements sound like your life? Is your schedule so crammed with homework, sports, and activities that you can't remember the last time you read your Bible or even where exactly you left your Bible? The world wants you to believe that you don't have time for God. And Satan loves to make you so busy that you don't even have time to talk to Him. But Jesus is great at multiplying—and that includes your time! No, He won't add hours to your day, but if you take time to make your relationship with Him important, you'll find there's always enough time for what's truly important.

*Heavenly Father, I always make time for
what's important to me. I want You to be
my number one priority. Today I want to
talk to You about _____. Amen.*

Master Crafted

*"I have called you by name. You are Mine! . . .
For I am the Lord your God, the Holy One of
Israel, Who saves you. . . . You are of great worth
in My eyes. You are honored and I love you."*

Isaiah 43:1, 3–4

Some incredible artists have painted priceless master-pieces that are worth a fortune. To date, the world's most expensive "priceless" painting is Leonardo da Vinci's *Salvator Mundi*. It sold in 2017 for 450 million dollars. Whoa!

Did you know that you were crafted by the Master Creator—the God of the whole universe? He shaped every part of you—how you look, your unique personality, your special talents and interests. And God says you are of great worth to Him. He loves you because you belong to Him.

Just like those priceless paintings on display in museums, your value comes from the One who made you. Because you were created by God, you are worthy. You are loved.

*Lord, thank You that I am valuable
because I am Your masterpiece. Amen.*

Help Out

Remember to do good and help each
other. Gifts like this please God.
HEBREWS 13:16

- -

Admit it. You still get excited about Christmas. What's
not to love when there are cookies, presents, and no
school? But usually the best gifts don't come in a box
or even cost you a dime. God says to help each other.
Does your elderly neighbor need some leaves raked or
the sidewalk shoveled? Does your mom need a hand
with the dinner dishes when she's tired? Or maybe your
grandma just wants to visit with you and chat. You can
give fantastic gifts even when you're low on funds.
Make friends with the new kid. Collect food for a food
bank. Do your chores without complaining. Fold a load
of laundry. Deliver cards to a nursing home. God loves
it when you're kind. And you'll feel great too.

God, help me not to be selfish with my money
or my time. Show me who needs my help
today. In Jesus' name, amen.

Pray Like Jesus

"Father, if it can be done, take away what must happen to Me. Even so, not what I want, but what You want."
LUKE 22:42

It's true that God may not always give us what we pray for. Disappointment can be hard to deal with. But remember that sometimes the things you ask for might hurt you or someone else. Or maybe you had a selfish attitude when you were praying. You can ask for things that are totally good, but maybe God—because He's amazingly wise—has a different plan. Sometimes He says to wait. He wants us to learn to trust Him. And sometimes God answers with yes and blesses us with something amazing just because He loves us. He will always listen and answer your prayers. Ask Him to teach you about His plan for you when He says no or wait.

Heavenly Father, help me want what You want for my life. Today I'm asking for _____, but I understand it might not be part of Your plan for me. Help me trust Your goodness and wisdom. Amen.

What to Pray For?

*First of all, I ask you to pray much for all men
and to give thanks for them. Pray for kings
and all others who are in power over us so
we might live quiet God-like lives in peace.*

1 TIMOTHY 2:1–2

- - - - - - - - - - - - - - - - - -

Not sure who or what to pray about? Just look around you. You can pray for the people you care about, like your parents, grandparents, siblings, and friends. You can pray for people in need, like missionaries that your church supports, your pastor, and your Sunday school teachers. You can pray for people who have been elected to lead, like judges, senators, our president, and school board members. Make a list so you can pray for them often. And don't forget to pray for yourself, that God will help you grow in wisdom and in your faith. Pray for Him to teach you more about Him.

*Lord, thank You for always being there
for me. Today I want to pray for
_____. In Jesus' name, amen.*

So Big!

"But who is able to build a house for Him? For the heavens and the highest heavens are not big enough to hold Him. So who am I, that I should build a house for Him, except as a place to burn special perfume before Him?"

2 CHRONICLES 2:6

- - - - - - - - - - - - - - - - - - -

As much as you might wish it could be true, you can't be in two places at once. God created us with physical bodies that are limited by time and space. So it's natural to wonder how God can be everywhere in the universe at once. But remember that God is spirit and not a person. He is all-powerful and doesn't have the same limits that we do. He can do anything—and that includes being everywhere at the same time just because He wants to. It's nice to know this about Him though. It means He is always there to love and help you.

Heavenly Father, it makes me feel really good to know that You are always close by—that I'm never alone. In Jesus' name, amen.

Getting It Right

The gifts on an altar that God wants are
a broken spirit. O God, You will not hate a
broken heart and a heart with no pride.

PSALM 51:17

- - - - - - - - - - - - - - - - - - - -

How can you please God with your prayers? Are there things He doesn't like? Should you pray a certain way? God does want you to be sincere when you pray—that means you don't use flowery words that don't mean anything to you. Just tell Him what really matters to you. Don't pray only at mealtimes or in church. He loves it when you find a quiet place and pray to Him all by yourself every day. (When you're all alone, you aren't trying to impress anyone either.) And God wants you to be respectful when you pray. Don't act like prayer doesn't matter or ask for silly things. Treat God like the loving, powerful Creator of the universe and King of kings that He is.

Lord, I want to please You with my prayers.
Help me be honest and respect You for the
awesome God that You are. Amen.

Avoiding Envy

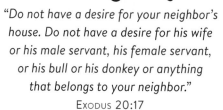

"Do not have a desire for your neighbor's house. Do not have a desire for his wife or his male servant, his female servant, or his bull or his donkey or anything that belongs to your neighbor."
EXODUS 20:17

- - - - - - - - - - - - - - - - - -

You probably don't want your neighbor's donkey, but at least one of your friends probably has something super cool (like the latest gaming system) that you totally wish was yours. Sometimes you might think having that thing will make you happy. God wants to know what's on your mind, but He also knows that having stuff isn't going to make you truly happy or feel filled-up inside. Instead, obeying God and living His way will bring true joy into your life. Trust God. Ask Him to provide what you need. And ask Him to help you be thankful and content with all the awesome things you already have.

God, I know that I don't need _____, but it would be nice. I'm so thankful for _____ that You've already given me. Amen.

Hand in Hand

*Now the God Who helps you not to give up
and gives you strength will help you think so
you can please each other as Christ Jesus
did. Then all of you together can thank the
God and Father of our Lord Jesus Christ.*
ROMANS 15:5–6

- -

You might have been in a situation where your pastor or Sunday school teacher asked you to hold hands while you were praying. And maybe that seemed a little strange, and you wondered why you should—or if you have to hold hands during prayer. Sometimes holding hands helps people feel closer. After all, we are all part of God's family, and He asks us to love and help each other. It can also show that you all agree as you pray for something.

*Lord, help me show love to other believers in Jesus.
I want to help them and pray together with them
about their problems. In Jesus' name, amen.*

Kids Welcome

Then little children were brought to Him that He might put His hands on them and pray for them. The followers spoke sharp words to them. But Jesus said, "Let the little children come to Me. Do not stop them. The holy nation of heaven is made up of ones like these."
MATTHEW 19:13–14

- - - - - - - - - - - - - - - - - -

Jesus had some sharp words for people who tried to keep children from coming to Him. He wants to know you and talk to you as well. You don't need to pray only with an adult or your parents. You can talk to God anytime. He loves to speak with His children, and He waits for your next prayers. Practice praying to God by yourself. Just tell Him what you've been thinking or worrying about. You don't need big words or fancy speeches; just talk to Him like you do your friends. He understands, and He can even teach you how to pray better.

Heavenly Father, I'm so glad I can trust You with my private concerns. Today I want to talk to You about _____. In Jesus' name, amen.

Do Life His Way

Jesus said, "I am the Way and the Truth and the Life. No one can go to the Father except by Me."

JOHN 14:6

- - - - - - - - - - - - - - - - -

Jesus said, "I am the Way." And He is! Knowing and loving Him is the only way to get to God. But Jesus also showed you the way to do things by the example that He set. Open your Bible to the New Testament, and read about how Jesus loved and talked to others. Think about how you can live your life more like He lived. He took time for people. And He considered what other people needed. Is there a chunk of your life that needs to look more like Jesus?

Heavenly Father, help me do life the way that Jesus did. I want to follow His example. He is the way to live. Today I want to be more like Jesus by _____. In Jesus' name, amen.

I'm Just Here for Jesus

O man, He has told you what is good.
What does the Lord ask of you but to do
what is fair and to love kindness, and to
walk without pride with your God?

MICAH 6:8

Have you seen the T-shirts that say "I'm just here for the dessert"? Pie, ice cream—if it's chocolate, I'm there! But have you ever asked yourself, "What am I here for?" Remember that we're not just here for good times, fun, and entertaining ourselves. God designed us with purpose and placed us here. We're here to live like Jesus. We're here to love God and love others. We're here to worship God. We're here to tell others about Him and how He's changed our lives.

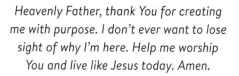

Heavenly Father, thank You for creating
me with purpose. I don't ever want to lose
sight of why I'm here. Help me worship
You and live like Jesus today. Amen.

Don't Worry—Pray!

Do not worry. Learn to pray about everything. Give thanks to God as you ask Him for what you need. The peace of God is much greater than the human mind can understand. This peace will keep your hearts and minds through Christ Jesus.

PHILIPPIANS 4:6-7

School, sports, homework, clubs, friends—your schedule is packed. And sometimes stress and anxiety attack even when you're having fun. The newness and change of growing up can be scary and stressful too.

But the apostle Paul wrote that you shouldn't worry about anything. Not. One. Thing. Why? Because you can have peace in your heart when you trust that God has some pretty amazing power. So how can you trade your worry for peace in the middle of this busy, scary life? Pray about everything, and ask God to take care of what you need. He'll help you! And don't forget to say thanks for what He's already done for you.

God, today I want to give my worry about _____ to You. I trust You. Amen.

A Friend When You're Sad

We give thanks to the God and Father of our Lord Jesus Christ. He is our Father Who shows us loving-kindness and our God Who gives us comfort. He gives us comfort in all our troubles.

2 CORINTHIANS 1:3–4

What do you do when you're feeling sad? Do you play sports or watch a funny TV show? Eat some chocolate or hug your mom? Have you ever asked God to heal your pain? He can help you no matter what kind of trouble you're in. If you think that no one understands your sadness. . .He does. Jesus knows all about pain. He was mocked, betrayed by His friends, beaten, and killed. People He loved died. And He saw others who were hurting and sick. He can understand your sadness and hurt too.

Pray and tell Jesus how you feel. Ask Him to help your pain. And you can talk to your parents or another grown-up too.

Jesus, I'm so glad You understand how I feel.
Help heal my hurt and sadness. Amen.

93

Love in Action

Love is kind. Love is not jealous. Love does not put itself up as being important. Love has no pride. Love does not do the wrong thing. Love never thinks of itself. Love does not get angry. Love does not remember the suffering that comes from being hurt by someone.

1 CORINTHIANS 13:4–5

- - - - - - - - - - - - - - - - - -

You know that God wants you to love people, right? But what does that mean? You feel love for your mom and dad. But how can you feel that way about *everyone*. . . even people you just met or don't like? God's kind of love isn't just a feeling—it's the way you treat people. The Bible says that you love others by being kind, forgiving, and thinking about other people first. So you don't need gushy feelings to love; just treat other people the way Jesus did.

God, sometimes showing love is really hard. Some people aren't very nice to me. But I also know that You want me to be kind. Today I need Your help to show love to _____. Amen.

When You Mess Up

*If we tell Him our sins, He is faithful and we
can depend on Him to forgive us of our sins.
He will make our lives clean from all sin.*

1 JOHN 1:9

- -

Have you ever prayed something like "God, I'm sorry for
all the things I did wrong today. Please forgive me. And
could You also forgive me for all the times I'm going to
mess up tomorrow too?" Sin is something we all have
to battle against daily. We're going to make mistakes.
Probably every day. But when we ask God to forgive
us, He does! Confessing means that we tell God what
we've done wrong, agree that it's sin, and ask Him to
forgive us. No one can forgive sins except God, so we
need to confess them to Him. And He promises that
when we confess, He will always forgive us.

*God, I really messed up today. I need to confess
_____ to You. Please forgive me. I know it was
wrong. Help me do the right thing in the future. Amen.*

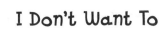

I Don't Want To

"I say to you who hear Me, love those who work against you. Do good to those who hate you. Respect and give thanks for those who try to bring bad to you. Pray for those who make it very hard for you."
LUKE 6:27–28

- -

Romans 12:20 says being kind to someone who has not been nice to you is like pouring burning coals onto their head. That means that if you pay back the bad someone has done to you with good, they will be ashamed of their behavior. And praying for kids who have been mean to you is one of the best ways you can help them. Pray that God would help you be kind to them so they can see God's love through you. If you have bad feelings toward them for hurting you, ask God to comfort your pain and change your heart. Forgiving them doesn't mean what they did was okay; it was still wrong.

God, my feelings are hurt, and I don't feel like praying for _____. Please change my heart and help me treat them with kindness. Amen.

Is Faith Blind?

Men cannot say they do not know about God. From the beginning of the world, men could see what God is like through the things He has made. This shows His power that lasts forever. It shows that He is God.
ROMANS 1:20

- - - - - - - - - - - - - - - - - - -

You've probably heard people talk about blind faith. What they really mean is believing in God without seeing Him—after all, He's invisible. So how are we supposed to know that He's actually there? When you get close to God, you'll see that your faith isn't really blind at all. You can see with your heart and mind that God is real. He's all around you, just like the wind. You can't see it, but you can see what it does during a storm! When you start praying and looking for God's help, you'll see how He changes your life.

Heavenly Father, I know that You are there. I trust in You. Help me see how You're working in my life. Today I need Your help with _____. Amen.

Unique Purpose

A heart that has peace is life to the body, but wrong desires are like the wasting away of the bones.

PROVERBS 14:30

- - - - - - - - - - - - - - - - - - -

Comparing yourself to other people can be a dangerous hobby. It's way too easy to look at other people and think that they have better stuff, look better, or play sports better. The Bible says these kinds of jealous thoughts are like rotten bones! God—who loves you—took time to create you with unique talents, and He wants you to use the gifts He's given you for Him. Today, instead of wishing you could be someone else, thank God for His creativity in making you different. What are you good at? Maybe you're great at making friends or you love to help people. Pray about how you can use those talents for God.

God, thank You for making me. . .well, me! Help me not to allow jealousy into my life, and show me how I can use my strengths for You. Amen.

Stage Fright

*I will make Your name known to
my brothers. In the center of the
meeting of worship I will praise You.*
PSALM 22:22

- - - - - - - - - - - - - - - - - - - -

Some people feel awkward praying out loud because
they're shy and afraid of saying the wrong thing or
getting laughed at. But you shouldn't feel ashamed or
embarrassed to pray in front of other people. You can
practice by praying out loud over family meals. Remember that praying isn't about impressing other people—it's
about talking to God. You don't have to try to show off
by using big words or trying to sound important. Just
talk to Him in your own words, from the heart.

*Heavenly Father, I get a little nervous when I have
to pray in front of other people. Help me remember
that I'm just talking to You. You just want to hear
what's on my heart. Keep my prayers humble so I
don't try to show off in front of others. Amen.*

What about the Small Stuff?

*But as one of them was cutting a tree, the ax
head fell into the water. The man cried out,
"It is bad, sir! The ax belongs to another man,
and I was to return it." The man of God said,
"Where did it fall?" And when he showed him
the place, Elisha cut off a stick and threw it
in, and the iron came to the top of the water.*

2 KINGS 6:5–6

- - - - - - - - - - - - - - - - - - - -

You might wonder if it's okay to pray to God about little
things that go wrong in your life. After all, He's a big,
powerful God with lots of things to pay attention to,
including people who have bigger problems than your
lost shoe. But God cares about you, even the small stuff.
Prayer isn't a substitute for learning to be responsible
with your things. But when little things go wrong, there's
no job He thinks is too small. He loves you!

*God, I know it seems like a little thing, but I really need
Your help with _____ . Thank You for caring
about every part of my life. In Jesus' name, amen.*

Down in My Heart

I pray that Christ may live in your hearts by
faith. I pray that you will be filled with love.
EPHESIANS 3:17

- - - - - - - - - - - - - - - - - - - -

It can be confusing when people say things like "get saved" and "ask Jesus into your heart." Really what they're trying to say is that you've decided to believe in and follow Jesus. It means that you want Him to be in charge of your life. You believe that He died for you to take the punishment for your sins and rose again three days later. And now He lives with God, preparing an amazing place for you. The Bible says that when you trust Jesus as your Savior by confessing your sins, asking His forgiveness, and telling Him that you want to do things God's way, the Holy Spirit then lives within you. Have you chosen to believe in Jesus?

Heavenly Father, I believe that Jesus died on the
cross for my sins. I know that I've done wrong things,
and I ask You to forgive me. I want to follow You,
God, for the rest of my life. In Jesus' name, amen.

When's a Good Time?

I thank God for you. I pray for you night and day. I am working for God the way my early fathers worked. My heart says I am free from sin.

2 TIMOTHY 1:3

Does God care what time of day you pray? Is it bad if you miss your bedtime prayer? There's no set time that God expects you to pray. But prayer is a good habit. God wants you to chat with Him every day and talk to Him all the time. Lots of people pray at bedtime or in the morning because they know that prayer is important to their relationship with God, and these times help them not to forget. Pick a time in your day when you can be consistent and concentrate on talking to God.

Heavenly Father, help me be consistent in my prayer time every day. I know I will have a better relationship with You if I talk to You often. Today I want to talk to You about _____. Amen.

Can Everyone Pray?

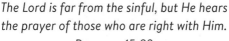

The Lord is far from the sinful, but He hears the prayer of those who are right with Him.
PROVERBS 15:29

- - - - - - - - - - - - - - - - - - - -

God doesn't stop anyone from praying. He says that all are welcome to come to Him. But there are some people in this world who don't want anything to do with God or His ways. They may even brag about the wrong things that they do. They don't pray because they don't want to talk to God and don't think that they need Him. They may not even believe that He exists. God knows that in their hearts they don't want a relationship with Him and that their prayers are just meaningless words. If these people want God to welcome their prayers, they need to admit their wrongs, turn from their ways, and ask for God's forgiveness.

Heavenly Father, I want to be right with You. I want You to see that in my heart I want to be more like Jesus. Today I need to confess _____ to You. In Jesus' name, amen.

Live Well

"Do what is right and good in the eyes of the Lord. Then it will be well with you."
DEUTERONOMY 6:18

- -

When you're a kid, people are always telling you, "Don't do that!" On the other hand, the world around you says to just do what feels good. So you might wonder why you should do what God says. But the Bible isn't just a book filled with a bunch of rules. Remember that God loves you more than you could ever imagine. He doesn't want to trick you or turn you into a robot. He wants only the best for you. In fact, He sent Jesus to die for you because of His awesome love. He doesn't want you to miss out on the good stuff He has in store for you because you're doing wrong. You can be sure that your life will go better when you do things God's way—be kind, love others, and forgive. Ask God what you need to work on to live His way.

God, show me where my attitude or actions need some work. In Jesus' name, amen.

Sweet News!

We thank God for the power Christ has given us. He leads us and makes us win in everything. He speaks through us wherever we go. The Good News is like a sweet smell to those who hear it.

2 CORINTHIANS 2:14

Mmm! The sweet smell of waffles brings you scurrying to the kitchen. The Bible says that the good news of Jesus is just like a sweet smell. When you tell people about Jesus' love for them, it sounds so good they'll want to know more—just the way those waffles make your mouth water for more! The awesome news that Jesus loves us and died on the cross for our sins so we could live in heaven with Him forever is called the Gospel or the Good News. Pray about who you can share the sweet news of Jesus with today.

Heavenly Father, I'm so happy that You've forgiven me! I know that some people don't know about You and how much You love them. Show me someone today who needs to know about Jesus, and help me know what to say. In Jesus' name, amen.

Keep Me from Sin

"Do not let us be tempted,
but keep us from sin."
MATTHEW 6:13

The apostle Paul said it pretty well: "I do not understand myself. I want to do what is right but I do not do it. Instead, I do the very thing I hate" (Romans 7:15). We all sin. Ever since Adam and Eve chose to sin in the Garden of Eden, we've all had to battle with our desire to do what is wrong. That's why we need God's help. He wants to help you, and He's the only one with the power to help you resist temptation. Remember: Not every impulse you have is a good one. When the disciples asked Jesus about prayer, He told them to pray, "Do not let us be tempted, but keep us from sin." Try it today!

Heavenly Father, please help me not to give in to sin. I don't want to choose wrong, but sometimes it's a very real battle. I especially need Your help with _____. In Jesus' name, amen.

Do I Need This?

I know how to get along with little and how to live when I have much. I have learned the secret of being happy at all times. If I am full of food and have all I need, I am happy. If I am hungry and need more, I am happy. I can do all things because Christ gives me the strength.
PHILIPPIANS 4:12–13

- - - - - - - - - - - - - - - - - - -

We all wish sometimes that we had stuff that we don't truly need. God promises to take care of the things that we need, but it isn't wrong to pray about things that we want. God wants you to be honest with Him about your feelings. But realize that we all want things that may not end up being the best for our lives. Like the apostle Paul, it's important to accept God's wisdom and answers and be content with the things He blesses us with.

Heavenly Father, I would really like to have _____ in my life. But I trust Your wisdom. In Jesus' name, amen.

Not Really Feelin' It

You must keep praying. Keep
watching! Be thankful always.
COLOSSIANS 4:2

- - - - - - - - - - - - - - - - - - - -

Have you ever prayed just because your parents said that you had to, but you didn't really feel like it? Remember that prayer is a good habit. If your parents made you brush your teeth every night before bed when you were little, you probably don't even think too much about it now; you just do it. Your parents are trying to help you develop the habit of prayer too. After all, if you only brushed when you felt like it, you probably wouldn't have teeth too long. Sometimes our feelings try to get in the way of what's good for us. And God rewards people who discipline themselves by praying often. God can work to change you for the better when you talk to Him often.

Lord, I want to do what's best for me,
even when I don't feel like it. Help me be
more diligent in my prayer times. Amen.

When God Says Yes!

Give thanks to the Lord for He is good!
His loving-kindness lasts forever! Let the
people who have been saved say so. He
has bought them and set them free from
the hand of those who hated them.

PSALM 107:1–2

- - - - - - - - - - - - - - - - - - - -

What if you pray about something—big or small—and God answers? Don't forget to thank Him for answering your prayer! Tell Him thanks for being such a good God and loving you so well. And tell others about it so they can see how great God is too. You can even make a list of all the things you've prayed about and how God answered your prayers. It can really encourage you to look back when you're feeling a little down and see how much God loves you. God is so awesome, it's impossible to run out of things to talk to Him about.

Lord, thanks for answering my prayer
about _____. It makes me feel loved
to know that You care and listen. Today I
want to pray for _____. Amen.

Give Him All You've Got

"You must love the Lord your God with all your heart and with all your soul and with all your mind and with all your strength."

MARK 12:30

- -

Take a moment and think about the thing that you love to do. Is it playing soccer, riding horses, drawing, or playing video games? Does thinking about this activity take up a lot of your mind and heart? Do you daydream about saddling your horse or imagine the perfect bicycle kick into the goal? You probably spend as much time as you can doing the thing that you love.

God wants this kind of devotion from you too—that you'll love Him with everything you've got. Why? Because He is worthy! He is the Creator of this world—and you. Tell Him today how awesome He is.

Father, thank You for loving me. Thank You for being the good God that You are. I want to love You today with all my heart, mind, soul, and strength. Show me how I can love You more. Amen.

Kindness Wins

The king said, "Is there not still someone of the family of Saul to whom I may show the kindness of God?" And Ziba said to the king, "There is still a son of Jonathan who cannot walk because of his feet."
2 SAMUEL 9:3

In Bible times, the winning king would usually get rid of the losing king's family. But King David was different. He was kind instead. King Saul had tried to kill David, but when David learned that Saul's grandson was crippled, David took care of him. If someone is mean to you, you might want to be mean right back. But God can help you be different like David; He can help you show kindness even when others don't. Pray about who you can show kindness to today.

Lord, thank You for being kind to me! I know that if I am kind to others, they will see Your love in me. Show me who needs to see Your kindness today. Help me be kind even if they haven't been kind to me. Amen.

Not Too Young

Let no one show little respect for you because you are young. Show other Christians how to live by your life. They should be able to follow you in the way you talk and in what you do. Show them how to live in faith and in love and in holy living.
1 TIMOTHY 4:12

You've probably heard the words "you're too young" more often than you like. But guess what? You're not too young to work for God! The Bible says that you can work for Jesus no matter how young you are. You can be kind and choose encouraging words that please God. You can love others by helping out—and doing it with a happy heart! Other people will see your good example and learn how to live for God too! Pray about how you can work for God today.

Heavenly Father, show me the work You want me to do for You today. Help me show others what is right by the good choices I make. Amen.

When You Have a Bad Day

In everything give thanks. This is what God wants you to do because of Christ Jesus.

1 THESSALONIANS 5:18

- -

You might wonder how you're supposed to give thanks when you've had a terrible day and nothing has gone right. The Bible doesn't say that you should thank God *for* every bad thing that happens to you; it says you should give thanks *in* everything. That means that in the midst of bad things, you can still thank God. Thank Him for being good, for loving you, and for having things under control. You can even tell Him what happened and how you're feeling about it. Tell Him you know that He is good and willing to help you. And thank Him for always being there for you. Praising God is a great way to get your mind off your problems.

Heavenly Father, today was not that great. I'm having a hard time because _____ . But I know that You're right here with me and will help me. I'm so glad that You've got this, God. Amen.

Keep Trying

*Do not give up. And as you wait
and do not give up, live God-like.*
2 PETER 1:6

- - - - - - - - - - - - - - - - - - - -

Think back to when you were learning how to catch a ball or write your name. Maybe you thought you'd never get it right. But it doesn't feel impossible now, does it? All that practice has paid off, and you just do it. Doing the right thing is a lot like learning a new skill—it takes practice. The more you choose to do what's right—like being kind, or obeying your parents right away, or being patient with others—the easier it becomes to make good choices. We all mess up sometimes, so don't be discouraged and don't give up. Just keep practicing doing what's right. And pray for God to help you too!

Heavenly Father, thank You for loving me and showing me how to live right. Please forgive me when I mess up, and help me keep trying to do right. Today I could really use Your help with _____. Amen.

Stand Out

God has given each of you a gift. Use it to help each other. This will show God's loving-favor.
1 PETER 4:10

Is there something about yourself that you really dislike—something that makes you stand out from everyone else when you'd rather just blend in? Maybe it's your glasses or your braces or your skin color, or maybe you snort when you laugh. Whatever it is, it's easy to feel sensitive about what sets you apart. But remember that God designed you to be you. He has given you traits and a personality unlike anyone else in the world. And you can't accomplish great things for Him by being the same as everyone else! Pray about the differences God put in your design. Ask Him to show you how you can use them to glorify Him.

Heavenly Father, I know that You made me unique. Help me see my differences as strengths instead of weaknesses. Bring other kids with differences into my life so I can encourage them too. Amen.

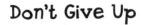

Don't Give Up

*Jesus told them a picture-story to show
that men should always pray and not
give up. . . . "Will not God make the things
that are right come to His chosen people
who cry day and night to Him? Will He
wait a long time to help them?"*
LUKE 18:1, 7

- - - - - - - - - - - - - - - - - -

Have you ever prayed and prayed about something, but
you didn't get the answer you were hoping for? What
should you do if it seems like God doesn't hear or answer
your prayers? You should keep praying. God understands
how you feel—after all, He created emotions. If you're
feeling discouraged, you should tell Him about it. And
tell Him that you trust Him and know He is good and
won't ever leave you or give up on you. Don't blame
God when you have problems or unanswered prayers.
God is always teaching you, and He may be using this
situation to make your faith stronger. Keep praying!

*God, help me see how You are using this tough
situation to teach me more about You. Amen.*

What's a Prayer Journal?

*Remember the great and powerful
works that He has done. Keep in mind
what He has decided and told us.*

PSALM 105:5

- -

Keeping a prayer journal is a great way to grow your faith in God. Usually people write down the things that they've been praying for and how God has answered their prayers. In the Old Testament, God told the Israelites not to forget how He'd delivered them from slavery in Egypt and parted the Red Sea so they could escape Pharaoh's army. God wanted their children to know about it too. When you remember the good things God has done for you, it's encouraging and helps you praise and thank God for His care. And when you look back and see how God has taken care of you before, it can help you be more patient for something you're praying about right now.

Lord, thank You so much for answering my prayer about _____. Help me not to forget all the good things You've done for me. In Jesus' name, amen.

When Someone Dies

*The death of His holy ones is of great
worth in the eyes of the Lord.*
PSALM 116:15

- -

What if you've prayed for someone not to die, but they did? Does that mean that your faith was too small or that God doesn't love that person? No, it absolutely doesn't. Everyone will die one day. And death doesn't mean that people weren't loved by God or didn't have enough faith. God tells us that He loves us all and sent Jesus to die on the cross for our sins. God has unlimited wisdom too. We have to trust His timing in numbering our days here on earth. But the amazing thing is that our life here isn't all there is. When we believe in Jesus, we will live with Him forever in heaven. Jesus said that He was going there to prepare an amazing place for us.

*Lord, it hurts when someone dies and I miss
them. But I trust You and Your goodness.
I look forward to seeing Jesus and all the
past believers in heaven someday. Amen.*

Watch Your Words

Watch your talk! No bad words should be coming from your mouth. Say what is good. Your words should help others grow as Christians.

EPHESIANS 4:29

- - - - - - - - - - - - - - - - - - - -

They say that "sticks and stones may break my bones but words can never hurt me." It's a nice thought, but if anyone has ever said something mean or teased you, you know how much words actually *can* hurt. God wants us to be very careful about the words we say, because He knows we can really hurt each other by saying unkind things. He has a different job for your words! God says to build others up and encourage them with your words instead of tearing people down. Pray about the words you use today. Ask God to help you say only encouraging and helpful things. Use your words to bring people closer to Jesus.

God, show me when my words are not helpful. Put kind and encouraging words in my mouth today. I could really use Your help when I'm talking to _____. Amen.

Stay Watchful

He said to them, "Why are you sleeping?
Get up and pray that you will not be tempted."
LUKE 22:46

- - - - - - - - - - - - - - - - - - - -

Your parents might tell you to say your bedtime prayers, but sometimes you're really tired because you've had a busy day, and you wonder if God will be upset if you're too tired to pray. Jesus asked His disciples to pray the night He was arrested. But He came back to find them snoozing. It's hard to pray when you're tired, but it's important to be in the habit of praying, even if it's not always convenient. Don't let tiredness keep you from talking to God. If you find that you're always tired, try planning a prayer time earlier in the day.

Heavenly Father, I know You understand
that sometimes I get tired. Help me plan
times to pray when I'm awake. I love
talking to You. In Jesus' name, amen.

How Much Faith?

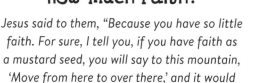

Jesus said to them, "Because you have so little faith. For sure, I tell you, if you have faith as a mustard seed, you will say to this mountain, 'Move from here to over there,' and it would move over. You will be able to do anything."

MATTHEW 17:20

Faith just means that you believe God is faithful and decide to trust that He is good and will do what He says. Jesus said that even if we have a tiny amount of faith, we can do amazing things in prayer. If you trust God even a little, He will do big things. To have great faith, we just need to trust God no matter what. Putting your trust in God means that you wait for Him instead of relying only on your own plans, strength, and smarts when you need help. Our God is mighty; try taking Him at His word today.

Heavenly Father, I trust that You are good and Your plans are best for me. Help my faith grow even more. In Jesus' name, amen.

How God Answers

*O God Who saves us, You answer us in
the way that is right and good by Your
great works that make people stand in
fear. You are the hope of all the ends of
the earth and of the farthest seas.*

PSALM 65:5

- -

After you pray for something, you might wonder what
kind of answers you should be looking for. Will there
be flashing lights and superheroes? Probably not, but
God is all-powerful, and He has limitless ways to answer
your prayers. He might use other people, like a doctor
to heal someone or a generous person to help out. He
might help you learn something about Him that changes
your thinking—so you think more like Jesus. And maybe
then those expensive shoes you wanted just won't
seem as important. He might say yes, no, or wait. Or
He might surprise you with how He takes care of you.

*Heavenly Father, I know You answer
prayer. Show me the ways You've helped
me in my life. In Jesus' name, amen.*

Others First

Jesus said to His followers, "If anyone wants to be My follower, he must forget about himself. He must take up his cross and follow Me."

MATTHEW 16:24

- -

Jesus taught us how to put others first. He didn't just give up His seat or share His dessert—He gave up His life for us. If you choose to follow Jesus, people should see you acting like Jesus would act. God can see your actions, but He can also see your thoughts—yes, even the selfish ones. Today, pray that God would show you the places in your life where you could be more selfless: places where you could put what others need in front of what you want, places where you could think more about how other people feel.

Lord, thank You for giving us Jesus as the best example of how to put others first. It can be so hard. Show me where I need to work on being less selfish in my life. In Jesus' name, amen.

He Loved You First

We love Him because He loved us first.
1 John 4:19

Think of the most difficult, hard-to-like person you know. Maybe it's someone who has hurt your feelings or gossiped about you. Now imagine that *you* are that person—the one who messes up all the time and sometimes does hurtful and wrong things. But guess what? Jesus loves you anyway! He knew you and loved you before you were even born. In fact, He came to earth to die for your sins long before you were alive. Think about it. He gave up His life for yours. Now that's true, unselfish love!

If you haven't accepted Jesus as your Savior, you can tell Him right now that you love Him too and want Him to forgive your sins and be part of your life. Know that you are loved today, and share His love with everyone you meet.

God, thank You for loving me first. I can't earn Your love or lose it because it's already mine forever. Amen.

It's a Win-Win!

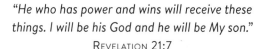

"He who has power and wins will receive these things. I will be his God and he will be My son."
REVELATION 21:7

- -

Doesn't it feel great to win? Whether it's sports or board games, who doesn't love the great feeling of winning? Did you know that God wants you to win too? The Bible tells us that through Jesus we have *already* won the victory! He won when He died on the cross for our sins. When you believe in Jesus and ask Him to forgive your sins, you become part of God's family. You win because the wrong things you have done no longer come between you and God. You win because the Holy Spirit now lives in you. You win because, as a child of God, you will live forever with Him in heaven.

Heavenly Father, thank You so much that I win through Jesus. Give me strength to do right and celebrate victory in Jesus. Today I need Your help with _____. In Jesus' name, amen.

When Someone Treats You Bad

"But I tell you, love those who hate you.
(Respect and give thanks for those who say
bad things to you. Do good to those who hate
you.) Pray for those who do bad things to you
and who make it hard for you. Then you may be
the sons of your Father Who is in heaven. His
sun shines on bad people and on good people.
He sends rain on those who are right with God
and on those who are not right with God."
MATTHEW 5:44–45

- - - - - - - - - - - - - - - - - -

Loving your enemies doesn't make sense to the world, but Jesus prayed for His enemies—including the ones who wanted Him to die. We need to pray for people who do wrong because they need prayer. They need to change and stop doing bad things. Remember, Jesus prayed for you too because He loved you even when you didn't yet follow Him.

Heavenly Father, today I need to pray
for _____. They need to know Your
love so they can stop doing wrong. Amen.

Study Up!

"This book of the Law must not leave your mouth. Think about it day and night, so you may be careful to do all that is written in it. Then all will go well with you. You will receive many good things."

JOSHUA 1:8

- - - - - - - - - - - - - - - - - - - -

How would you do on your next math test in school if you never opened your book? Probably not great, right? It's the same with following Jesus. How will you know what choices you should make or what behaviors will please God if you never open your Bible and read it? You won't!

The Bible says to study and think about God's directions all the time so you'll be careful to do what's right instead of what's wrong. Find your Bible and spend a few minutes reading. Learn what God has to say about living to please Him. He loves you so much and wants your life to go well!

Heavenly Father, show me the right way to live as I read Your Word. In Jesus' name, amen.

127

Tell the Truth

Do not lie to each other. You have put out of your life your old ways.
COLOSSIANS 3:9

- - - - - - - - - - - - - - - - - - -

Have you ever done something you knew was wrong. . .and then had to fess up? Was it hard? The Bible says that God hates lying but delights in those who tell the truth. He feels this way because lying hurts your relationships. It breaks trust. And broken trust is hard to fix.

Satan, your enemy, is the father of lies. He's ecstatic anytime you lie too. Next time you're thinking about bending the truth, ask yourself, "Who do I want as my father? The Father of truth or the father of lies?" Take off your old ways of doing things and put on new ones—God's good and perfect ways. And your heavenly Father will be delighted with you!

Father, give me strength to always tell the truth, no matter what. Show me any situations where I've been less than honest so I can fix it. In Jesus' name, amen.

More Than You Asked For

Praise the Lord, O my soul. And forget none of His acts of kindness. . . . He fills my years with good things and I am made young again like the eagle.

PSALM 103:2, 5

- - - - - - - - - - - - - - - - - -

You might think that God is only concerned with giving you the bare minimum. But He didn't create this big, beautiful world for nothing. He wants you to enjoy all that He made. And He can give you more than you hope for or imagine. Jesus said, "Would any of you fathers give your son a stone if he asked for bread? . . . You are sinful and you know how to give good things to your children. How much more will your Father in heaven give the Holy Spirit to those who ask Him?" (Luke 11:11, 13).

God, I'm so glad that You love me and find pleasure in blessing me with good things just so I can enjoy them and the amazing God who created them. Today I want to thank You for giving me _____. Amen.

Right Living

Man is helped when he is taught God's Word.
It shows what is wrong. It changes the way of
a man's life. It shows him how to be right with
God. It gives the man who belongs to God
everything he needs to work well for Him.
2 TIMOTHY 3:16–17

It's nearly impossible to put together a new bike without the instructions. You'll be clueless about what goes where or how to get it working right. The Bible is a lot like those directions. It tells you everything you need to know about who God is and what's right and wrong. And it also tells you how to live with God in heaven forever—by believing in Jesus and asking Him to forgive you.

Read your Bible right now! And pray for God's direction on how to live for Him!

Lord, thank You so much that You gave us the
Bible to teach us about doing what's right and
to teach us about You. Help me read my Bible
every day so I'm ready to work for You. Amen.

Love Hard

*"I give you a new Law. You are to
love each other. You must love each
other as I have loved you."*

JOHN 13:34

- - - - - - - - - - - - - - - - - -

What does it look like to love like Jesus? Jesus was kind, compassionate, and unselfish always, even when people weren't nice to Him. He forgave people who hurt Him— even those who nailed Him to the cross. And He was good to the difficult and hard-to-like people too. Being like Jesus means loving with everything you've got!

Whew! What a huge job! And loving like that all the time isn't easy—like speaking kindly to your little brother even though he lost your favorite ball glove or forgiving your friend for spilling your new nail polish.

Jesus showed us in the Bible how to love other people, no matter how they look or where they live. And He wants you to do the same! You *can* do it—with His help!

*Jesus, thank You for loving me all the
time, no matter what. Show me how to
love others like You love me. Amen.*

Overcomer

Do not let sin have power over you.
Let good have power over sin!
ROMANS 12:21

Bad things happen sometimes, even to good people. And it can seem as if the bad is always winning: bullies give you a hard time at school, someone stole your bike, and gossipers spread mean lies about people. But God has a plan for you to be an overcomer.

The Bible says that Jesus has gone before you—He's already overcome this world. He died so you could be free from sin instead of trapped by evil. And He wants your help in showing the world that good has power over evil.

Pray today and ask God to make you strong when you're tempted, even if people around you are choosing sin. Take a stand for what's right. Be an example of how kind words can overcome hurtful words. Show that putting others first can overpower selfishness. You can be an overcomer. . .with God's help.

Heavenly Father, today I need help to overcome
_____. In Jesus' name, amen.

Sweet Dreams

*The Lord will send His loving-kindness in
the day. And His song will be with me in
the night, a prayer to the God of my life.*
PSALM 42:8

You're telling your dad this great story about what happened today, and you look over, only to discover that he has fallen asleep in his recliner—right in the middle of your story! It doesn't feel good when someone nods off while you're talking to them, so you might wonder if God minds when you fall asleep while you're praying at night. It's always good to pray, and what an awesome way to fall asleep—in conversation with God. But it's great to set aside times when you're awake too, so you aren't distracted or groggy and can pray about important things.

*Heavenly Father, I love telling You about my
day. I'm glad that You don't mind if I fall
asleep talking to You. Today I want to tell You
about _____. In Jesus' name, amen.*

Servants First

"Whoever wants to be first among you, let him be your servant. For the Son of Man came not to be cared for. He came to care for others."
MATTHEW 20:27–28

If you grow up to be rich, you can afford to pay lots of people to do the jobs you don't really feel like doing, right? Well, in God's kingdom, being a part of the King's family doesn't mean you get the royal treatment. In fact, Jesus said that if you want to be first in His kingdom, you should follow His example and serve others. You might be wondering why you should live the very unglamorous life of a servant. We love others because of God's great and amazing love for us!

So how can you serve in God's kingdom today? It's very simple! Look around and see what someone needs. And then find out how to help. You can be kind, giving, and unselfish.

Lord, show me who I can serve today. Amen.

Sometimes God Says No

*Trust in the Lord with all your heart, and
do not trust in your own understanding.
Agree with Him in all your ways, and
He will make your paths straight.*

PROVERBS 3:5–6

Your parents don't always say yes when you ask them for something. And it can be really upsetting when you don't get what you want or think that you need. But your parents love you, and because they have a lot of experience, they can see when something might not be good for you or when you're just not ready for it. God doesn't always say yes either. But never think that He doesn't care. It's really the opposite: His great love for you and huge wisdom means He knows what's best. He has a plan for each person's life—including yours. Wait and trust in His love and wisdom.

*Lord, help me understand when You say no. Help me
see how the thing I'm asking for might not be the
best thing for me at this moment. I trust You. Amen.*

Sunshine or Rain

But our God is in the heavens.
He does whatever He wants to do.
PSALM 115:3

Have you ever wondered how God can handle people praying for opposite things? Farmers pray for rain, and ball players pray for sunshine—all at the same time. People on opposite sides of war pray for victory, and God loves people on both sides. We all need different things and pray for our concerns. But God can see everything and into the future. He has both the power and the wisdom to work all things out for the best— for everyone. God is infinite—that means He has no limits! You can thank Him today that He is wise and all-seeing.

Heavenly Father, I'm so glad that You are all-powerful and all-knowing. I trust in what You decide is best because I know that You've got this under control. In Jesus' name, amen.

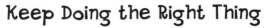

Keep Doing the Right Thing

Do not let yourselves get tired of doing good. If we do not give up, we will get what is coming to us at the right time. Because of this, we should do good to everyone. For sure, we should do good to those who belong to Christ.

GALATIANS 6:9–10

When you follow Jesus, you don't do the right thing because it's easy; you do it because it's right. You know you should finish your chores, but you really want to watch your favorite TV show instead. And you know that gossiping about one of your friends isn't right, but everyone else in your circle is joining in. Will you choose to stand up for what's right? Keep going! Don't get tired of choosing to do the right thing, even when it's hard. Making choices that are pleasing to God comes with rewards! Not only will you build good character, but you'll also pile up heavenly treasures.

Father, give me strength to do what's right even when it's so very hard. In Jesus' name, amen.

With My Whole Heart

*"These people show respect to Me with
their mouth, but their heart is far from Me."*
MATTHEW 15:8

If your mom asks you to clean your room and you stomp
off and complain as you do it, are you really obeying
her? Not so much, right? That's because your heart
wasn't in the right place.

Did you know that God sees your heart? It's true.
He can! So He knows if you have the right attitude. God
wants more than just saying the right thing at church;
He wants you to love Him with your whole heart. And
when you do, you'll have joy and want to please Him
by doing what's right. Ask God today to show you the
places in your heart where your attitude needs a little fix.

*God, I want You to see the real me, and I want
who I am to make You happy. Show me where I
haven't been obeying You with a happy heart and
help me fix my attitude. In Jesus' name, amen.*

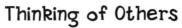

Thinking of Others

Nothing should be done because of pride or thinking about yourself. Think of other people as more important than yourself.

PHILIPPIANS 2:3

- - - - - - - - - - - - - - - - - - - -

Putting ourselves first comes naturally to us. It's super easy to forget about others and think only about what you want. But God tells us to think about other people first. When was the last time you put someone else first? Maybe you let one of your siblings choose what TV show to watch or shared some candy you'd much rather eat by yourself. Or maybe you helped your mom with the dishes when you wanted to play a video game instead. If you've done something selfless, awesome job! Keep up the great work. Pray today and ask God to show you more ways that you can put others first—just like He did. And don't forget to pray for others too, not just for your own needs.

Heavenly Father, it's hard not to be selfish sometimes. Show me how I can put someone else first. And show me who needs my prayers. Amen.

Filled with Joy!

Our hope comes from God. May He fill you with joy and peace because of your trust in Him.

ROMANS 15:13

Your team wins the championship game, and your parents take you out for ice cream to celebrate! You feel so great when things are going well for you. But what about when things go wrong? What about when you don't get something you really, really wanted so bad? Or one of your friends says something that hurts your feelings? You see, joy isn't just gushy good feelings when everything is good. Joy is something different. You can be joyful even in the hard times. The key is being thankful for the awesome things you've gained through Jesus. When you're feeling down, turn on some praise music, list all the good things God has given you, and ask Him to change your feelings. He'll show you all the reasons you have to be joyful!

God, thank You for _____ . Amen.

Big Problems

"The Lord will fight for you.
All you have to do is keep still."
EXODUS 14:14

- -

Have you ever had a big problem you knew you couldn't fix by yourself? One that maybe felt impossible? Well, the Israelites felt this way after they'd escaped from slavery in Egypt. They were backed up against the Red Sea with no way across—and Pharaoh's army was chasing them. It seemed like they were doomed. But nothing is impossible for God. He's bigger and more powerful than all your problems. When the Israelites thought they were trapped, God parted the sea so they could walk across on dry land. God will fight for you too. When you feel trapped, ask God to take over. Trust Him to care for you, and give all your worry to Him. You can rest, knowing that the powerful God who divided a sea can solve your problems.

God, I trust You. Please help me with
_____. In Jesus' name, amen.

Ask to Understand

*Try to understand other people. Forgive
each other. If you have something
against someone, forgive him. That
is the way the Lord forgave you.*

Colossians 3:13

- - - - - - - - - - - - - - - - - - - -

Have you ever been upset and then realized that you
didn't understand the whole story? Maybe you yelled
at your little brother for taking your new markers. . .and
then your mom told you he was making you a birthday
card. God wants you to have forgiveness in your heart.
He wants you to try to understand the problems other
people are having—and that always makes forgiveness
easier. After all, even though you're pretty awesome
in God's eyes, sometimes you need forgiveness too.
Next time you get upset with someone, stop and ask
God to give you understanding and forgiveness.

*God, thank You so much that You always understand
my pain and problems and that You always forgive me.
Help me care about others and try to understand
their problems instead of getting angry. Help
me always forgive. In Jesus' name, amen.*

With a Happy Heart

Whatever work you do, do it with all your heart. Do it for the Lord and not for men.
COLOSSIANS 3:23

- - - - - - - - - - - - - - - - - - -

Do you have lots of chores around the house? Maybe you fold your own laundry or take out the trash. Sometimes daily chores can feel like a drag. But part of growing up is learning responsibility—that means your parents can count on you. Growing up responsible, like most worthwhile things, is hard work. Sometimes you won't feel at all like getting to work. How do you respond when you'd rather play a video game or ride your bike? Do you grumble and put off your chores? Or do you power through with a can-do, positive attitude?

Remember that God wants you to do every job like you were doing it just for Him. Smile and put your best foot forward. Pray about how you can better work with a happy heart.

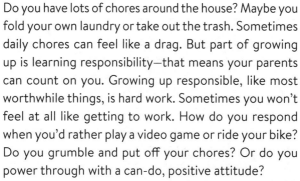

Lord, help me have a happy and willing heart as I finish every job. Today I need help doing _____ with a good attitude. Amen.

Happy and Humble

"Those who have no pride in their hearts are happy, because the earth will be given to them."
MATTHEW 5:5

What is something you're really good at? Did you ever feel like your talent for running fast, scoring goals, or being smart made you just a little more important than your friends? That sneaky feeling is called pride. And it's the opposite of how God wants you to behave. Jesus gave us a perfect example of humility—not thinking you're better than others. He's the Son of God, but He didn't think He was too good to serve others by washing their dirty feet.

Remember that every person you meet is just as valuable to God as you are. This thought will keep you thinking right about yourself and how you treat others.

Heavenly Father, keep me from becoming puffed up with pride. I know that I am precious to You, just like every person I'll meet today. Help me be more humble about my _____. Amen.

Tame Your Temper

A fool always loses his temper,
but a wise man keeps quiet.
PROVERBS 29:11

Do you lose your temper when you're angry? If someone really gets under your skin, do you say mean things? Or how about when your parents don't give you what you want? How do you react? Do you argue, yell, stomp to your room, and sulk?

God says you're wise to use your self-control, and when you're upset, it's even more important that you keep yourself under control. You can still obey your parents without a poor attitude and speak gently to others when you're upset. If you lose control and yell or slam the door, you're going to be sorry about it later. So before you open your mouth in anger today, stop and pray. Ask God to help you practice self-control by keeping those angry words quiet. You'll be so glad you did!

God, help me control my temper so I don't do
hurtful things to others. I really need Your help
using self-control when _____. Amen.

Again?

You must pray at all times as the Holy Spirit leads you to pray. Pray for the things that are needed. You must watch and keep on praying. Remember to pray for all Christians.

EPHESIANS 6:18

Have you ever thought that God needs a break or that He'll get tired of hearing the same prayers from you every day? Well, that's not true. You don't have to keep praying the exact same prayer every day (sometimes when you say the exact same thing over and over, it loses its meaning or your mind wanders while you're praying). But it is good to keep praying every day for things that are important or when you're waiting for an answer. God can use our repeated prayers to change us. He might show you that you need an attitude change, or He might open up a new solution that you never would have noticed. What important things do you need to keep bringing to God?

Father God, I'm so glad You never get tired of listening to me. Today I need to talk to You about _____. Amen.

You're Golden

"Do for other people whatever you would like to have them do for you."

MATTHEW 7:12

Someone says something mean or ignores you. What will you do? What do you think Jesus would want you to do? If you don't know what Jesus would say, you can find out by reading the Gospels, the first four books of the New Testament. Jesus got right to the point: treat other people the way that you like to be treated. And who doesn't prefer kindness to rudeness? It's not that hard to be nice to someone who's nice to you, but Jesus says to be kind to everyone—even the hard-to-like people. Sometimes mean kids are really just hurting kids. And maybe your gentleness will be the perfect Band-Aid for their pain. Pray about who might need a friend today.

Father, help me see the people around me who are hurting, and help me be kind even when they aren't, so I can show them the love of Jesus. Amen.

Show Some Gratitude

*Keep your lives free from the love of
money. Be happy with what you have.*
Hebrews 13:5

New things are fun. You've probably seen tons of ads on TV for stuff and then begged your parents to buy it for you. But the Bible warns us not to get all wrapped up in loving things that money can buy. God wants us to be grateful and happy with what we have. When you're so busy wanting all the things you don't have, you forget to enjoy what you do have. Being content lets you enjoy all the great things God has already given you. Next time you want something, stop and think about all the great things God has already given you—and then pray and thank Him for being so good to you.

*Heavenly Father, thanks for always being there for
me. And thanks for giving me so much. Today I want
to thank You especially for _____. Amen.*

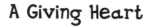

A Giving Heart

*Tell them to do good and be rich in
good works. They should give much to
those in need and be ready to share.*

1 Timothy 6:18

— — — — — — — — — — — — — — — — — —

Are you a sharer or a saver? Do you always know who
to share something with, or do you save your stuff for
a rainy day? God wants us to be generous with what
we have. After all, He is the One who gives us everything we need, and He wants us to pass it on! Try sharing
today. Be generous, and see how God will reward you
with blessings—even if that means the blessing of feeling good inside because you helped someone or brought
a smile to a face!

And don't forget that you can be generous with
your time too. Go help an elderly neighbor mow the
grass, or help your parents with extra chores. Ask God
how you can be generous today.

*Lord, thank You for all the good things You've
given me. Help me give back and help others. Amen.*

Live Free

*You were chosen to be free. Be careful
that you do not please your old selves
by sinning because you are free. Live this
free life by loving and helping others.*

<small>GALATIANS 5:13</small>

- - - - - - - - - - - - - - - - - - - -

A lot of people around you probably say that you should
do whatever makes you feel good. But now you know
Jesus and how much He loves you. He forgave you for
every wrong thing you've ever done and every wrong
word you've ever said. You're free from all that guilt!
You're free to be a brand-new you! But bad habits—
like thinking of yourself first—are hard to break.

Jesus wants you to use your freedom to love others
and help them. It might seem hard to stop acting like
the old you, but God will help if you ask.

Is there a bad habit you need to break? Ask God
for help right now.

*Father, help me break old habits that are wrong
and live free as I love others. Make me brave
and strong to love even when it's hard. Amen.*

Looks That Last

Do not let your beauty come from the outside. It should not be the way you comb your hair or the wearing of gold or the wearing of fine clothes. Your beauty should come from the inside. It should come from the heart. This is the kind that lasts. Your beauty should be a gentle and quiet spirit. In God's sight this is of great worth and no amount of money can buy it.
1 Peter 3:3–4

- -

The world says that how we look on the outside is really important. Be thin, muscular; wear the right clothing brands, the trendiest shoes. But the Bible tells us that God isn't as concerned with the outside. Sure, He designed you, but He looks more than skin deep. He sees your heart.

No matter what you look like on the outside, you can be beautiful to God. Someday you'll grow older and maybe your muscles will sag and your hair will turn gray, but the kind of beauty God sees is gentleness, kindness, and a calm and faithful trust in Him.

Lord, I want a spirit that pleases You. Amen.

Always Listening

I love the Lord, because He hears
my voice and my prayers.
PSALM 116:1

- - - - - - - - - - - - - - - - - - -

Did you know that no matter what time it is, God always hears your prayers? He does! Unlike your friends or your parents, who are sometimes distracted, God is always listening. And He'll never tell you to wait a minute. In fact, He wants to talk to you. Every day! All day!

The Bible says to pray continually—that means all the time. Praying is simply talking with God and listening for what He has to say back. It's a conversation with your Creator, who loves you very much.

You can talk to God about everything. Worried? Tell God about your fears, and ask Him for peace and trust. Confused? Ask God for wisdom. Lonely? Talk to Him—ask Him to send a friend your way. He hears and understands everything you need.

Father, I want to spend more time talking
to You—about everything. Today I want to
talk to You about _____. Amen.

Who Are You Trying to Impress?

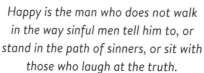

*Happy is the man who does not walk
in the way sinful men tell him to, or
stand in the path of sinners, or sit with
those who laugh at the truth.*

PSALM 1:1

- -

Have you ever done something because your friends were doing it, even though you knew it was wrong? Maybe you didn't want them to laugh at you or stop being your friend because you didn't join in. That's called peer pressure. But God says that you won't find joy by sinning right along with everyone else; you'll find joy by walking with Jesus and doing good!

God wants you to think about His ways all the time. That means reading your Bible every day and living like Jesus. Live to please God instead of your friends, and you will have true joy!

Heavenly Father, help me be strong to do the right thing, even when it's not popular. In Jesus' name, amen.

Mighty in Gentleness

A gentle answer turns away anger,
but a sharp word causes anger.

PROVERBS 15:1

Back in Bible times, God's people were waiting for a king to fight their enemies. But instead of fighting with people, Jesus said, "Learn from Me. I am gentle and do not have pride. You will have rest for your souls" (Matthew 11:29). Jesus was gentle, even with those who weren't nice. When someone makes fun of you or takes your stuff, it's hard not to get mad, right? But God says that using gentle words will help you—and others—keep your cool. Defeat anger with gentleness by asking God to help you speak calm words today.

Jesus, I'm so glad that You're a gentle but mighty
King. Teach me to control my tongue when I'm
angry. Please help me use gentle words with
_____ today. In Jesus' name, amen.

A Grateful Attitude

*Be glad you can do the things you
should be doing. Do all things without
arguing and talking about how you
wish you did not have to do them.*

PHILIPPIANS 2:14

- -

What do you say when your parents or a teacher asks you to do something you really don't want to do—like fold your laundry or do an extra page of math homework? Do you grumble? Complain? Whine? Argue? Or do you say, "Sure, I can do that!" Instead of wishing you didn't have to do some things and thinking about what you'd rather be doing, do what God says: try being thankful that you *can* do what you're asked.

It's super easy. Just pray, "Thank You, God, for giving me all these great clothes to wear," while you're doing laundry. Or "Thank You, God, that I get to go to school and learn when lots of kids in the world can't go to school." Try it today!

*Heavenly Father, show me how to be grateful instead of
grumbling. Thank You so much for _____. Amen.*

His Ways Are Higher

"For My thoughts are not your thoughts, and My ways are not your ways," says the Lord. "For as the heavens are higher than the earth, so are My ways higher than your ways, and My thoughts than your thoughts."

Isaiah 55:8–9

- - - - - - - - - - - - - - - - - -

Have you ever gotten lost in a corn maze? It's so frustrating to walk and walk, only to end up back where you started—and no closer to getting out! Sometimes God's answers to our prayers seem strange. We might think we really need something, but He says no or gives us something else instead. God is like a tall friend who can see over the corn rows and tell you which way to go. And He knows exactly what you need at any given time. Learn to trust in His goodness and love for you.

God, I know that You love me a lot and that You want the best for me. Sometimes it's hard when I don't get the answer I wanted. Help me trust You because You can see things I can't. Amen.

Can I Pray for My Pet?

A man who is right with God cares for his animal,
but the sinful man is hard and has no pity.
PROVERBS 12:10

- -

God created animals and loves them. And He also loves you. He wants you to pray about things that are important to you. If you have a pet that matters to you, He wants to hear your concerns. God shows His care for animals in the unique and creative ways that He designed them. And He gave us dominion over them and the responsibility to care for them. That means He cares about treating animals with kindness.

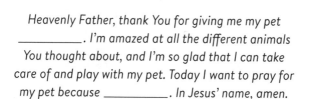

Heavenly Father, thank You for giving me my pet
_____. I'm amazed at all the different animals
You thought about, and I'm so glad that I can take
care of and play with my pet. Today I want to pray for
my pet because _____. In Jesus' name, amen.

Choose Right

"Watch and pray so that you will not be tempted. Man's spirit is willing, but the body does not have the power to do it."

MATTHEW 26:41

- - - - - - - - - - - - - - - - - -

"Look out!" Have you ever been saved from injury by a quick warning? Maybe you almost got hit by a baseball, but someone yelled, "Heads up!" Just like we watch out for danger, God says to watch out for temptation. You have to pay attention because temptation is sneaky. You might even think something bad looks really good— like telling a "white lie" to get out of trouble. We all mess up sometimes and choose to do what we know is wrong—like ignoring our parents. We can't resist all this temptation by ourselves; we need God's help! Ask God to give you power to do what's right.

Heavenly Father, thank You for sending us the Holy Spirit to help us. I don't want to fall for Satan's tricks. Help me watch out for sin and choose to do right so I don't disappoint You. In Jesus' name, amen.

158

Pray for Wise Friends

He who walks with wise men will be wise.
PROVERBS 13:20

- -

Most often the people we spend time with tend to rub off on us. When you're choosing your close friends, ask yourself, "Is it a wise choice to hang out with this person?" "Will this friend encourage me to follow Jesus?" You should stay away from people who do and say things that go against what the Bible teaches us is right, or they could lead you away from Jesus—and into harm. Choosing not to spend time with some people doesn't mean you think you're better than they are. God loves them too! And He died for their sins just like He died for yours. So pray for them to come to know Jesus. Pick friends who are kind, loving, joyful, compassionate, patient, and giving, and you will become more of those things too!

Lord, give me wisdom as I choose who to hang out with. Send me friends who love You. Amen.

Are You Listening, God?

I cried to the Lord in my trouble,
and He answered me.
PSALM 120:1

Sometimes you pray, and it seems like nothing is happening. Everything stays the same, and you wonder if God is doing anything to answer your prayer. But the Bible tells us that God listens and answers our prayers. You might not get the answer that you wanted, because God has greater wisdom. Whether His answer is yes, no, or wait, you can trust that it is the best thing for you. God cares the most about changing you to be more like Jesus—and He isn't your personal vending machine. Stay close to God through constant prayer, and your talks with Him will help you understand what He is doing for you. He wants to hear from you.

Heavenly Father, the Bible says that You're working to
answer my prayers. Help me become more like Jesus.
Show me what You want me to do today. Amen.

All Together

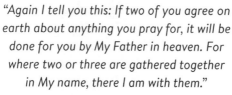

"Again I tell you this: If two of you agree on earth about anything you pray for, it will be done for you by My Father in heaven. For where two or three are gathered together in My name, there I am with them."
MATTHEW 18:19–20

- - - - - - - - - - - - - - - - - - -

Sometimes praying with other people can be a little uncomfortable. But God loves it when we pray together because we're showing our love and support for one another. God calls His church the body of Christ. He wants all the different parts of His body to work together. When you pray with others, you can make them stronger and encourage them. You can share your prayer requests with others and pray for each other. It's great to know that someone is praying for you! And together your prayers are more powerful.

Lord, show me who I can pray with and who needs my prayers and encouragement. Today I'd like to pray with _____. In Jesus' name, amen.

Kindness Counts

You must be kind to each other. Think of the other person. Forgive other people just as God forgave you because of Christ's death on the cross.

EPHESIANS 4:32

- -

Everyone knows that icky feeling of walking into a room full of other kids. . .but you don't know anyone there. You feel a little nervous and shaky, afraid no one will talk to you or be your friend. But then someone comes over and says hi and invites you to sit with him. Suddenly, your heart feels lighter. Doesn't it feel great when someone is kind to you?

Now think about how you could make other people feel that way inside too. All it takes is a little kindness. If you don't know how, remember: Just treat others the way you would like to be treated. And your kindness just might inspire your friends to be kind too. Pray about what acts of kindness God has for you to do today.

Heavenly Father, show me who needs my kindness today. Give me courage to be kind. Amen.

Wait for God

*But they who wait upon the Lord will get
new strength. They will rise up with wings
like eagles. They will run and not get tired.
They will walk and not become weak.*

Isaiah 40:31

- - - - - - - - - - - - - - - -

Waiting builds character. . .or so your mom says when
you're really excited for something good to happen.
But waiting is hard! Even grown-ups find it hard to wait.

When we wait for God, there's a pretty awesome
reward in it for us. God says that He'll do the work when
we follow His plans. Have you ever seen a picture of an
eagle soaring on the wind? It's like that when you wait
for God's plans to unfold and pray for His direction in
your life. He promises to make you strong and carry
you, just like the wind lifts the eagle.

*God, thank You for planning a great future for me.
Waiting is hard, especially when I want to do what I
want. Give me patience to wait for You and wisdom
to see Your plans. In Jesus' name, amen.*

Dress for Success

*God has chosen you. You are holy and
loved by Him. Because of this, your new
life should be full of loving-pity. You should
be kind to others and have no pride. Be
gentle and be willing to wait for others.*
COLOSSIANS 3:12

- - - - - - - - - - - - - - - - - - - -

I bet you've never hopped out of bed as your alarm beeps, scarfed down breakfast, headed out the door. . . and realized you forgot to get dressed! Clothes are kind of important, so I'm sure you never leave home without them. But there are some other important wardrobe pieces that God wants you to wear. Do you ever forget to put on your patience when you're getting ready for the day? Or how about your kindness? God thinks these good things are even more important than what you're wearing on the outside. Start every day right. Remember your most important accessories—compassion, kindness, humility, gentleness, and patience.

*Father, help me remember that my actions are
more important than my clothes. Today I need
Your help putting on _____. Amen.*

164

The Right Time

*There is a special time for everything. There is a
time for everything that happens under heaven.*
ECCLESIASTES 3:1

- - - - - - - - - - - - - - - - - -

Have you ever prayed for something and then wondered
why God wasn't answering your prayer. . .*right now,
please!*? It might seem like what you're praying for is
a great thing and definitely something that He should
say yes to. But remember that God knows more than
you do. He has way more wisdom than you could ever
imagine. And that means He knows the best time to
answer your prayers. Sometimes you don't even have to
wait—He answers before you say anything. Sometimes
He's waiting to use the people around you to answer your
prayers, and sometimes He knows that you aren't ready
for the thing that you want and need to grow a little
more. Keep trusting, and your faith will get stronger.

*Heavenly Father, give me patience and help me
grow stronger faith in Your goodness and wisdom.
Please help me trust You with _____. Amen.*

You Can Do It

I can do all things because
Christ gives me the strength.
PHILIPPIANS 4:13

- - - - - - - - - - - - - - - - - - -

The apostle Paul was locked in prison for telling people about Jesus when he wrote the words of Philippians 4:13. At times, doing what you know God says is right can be so very tough, especially when following Jesus means awful things might happen—like being made fun of or being left out. But this verse helps us remember that we're not alone in the hard times. Jesus sees when you're working for Him, and He will make you strong so you can keep doing the right thing.

How do you need Jesus to help you be strong in your life? Do you need His strength to keep a good attitude when you're doing chores? To obey your mom and dad when you'd rather not? To be kind?

Ask God to give you strength today in an area where you're struggling.

Heavenly Father, give me Your strength today,
and help me with _____. In Jesus' name, amen.

What Can You Share?

Nothing should be done because of pride or thinking about yourself. Think of other people as more important than yourself.

PHILIPPIANS 2:3

- - - - - - - - - - - - - - - - -

You score all the best candy from the prize bowl—*yes!* Then you see your little brother's sad face. You realize that having everything all to yourself doesn't make you feel good inside. After all, can you really be happy when you've done something that makes someone else feel bad? Sharing or giving up something that you totally want is hard, but the payoff comes with how great you'll feel inside. That's one reason why the Bible says to put others first instead of thinking only about yourself. Putting others first is also an awesome way to show God's love to other people. God shared His beautiful creation and—more importantly—His Son, Jesus, with us. Pray about how you too can share more.

God, thank You for sharing this beautiful world with me. Thank You for giving Jesus to us. Show me what I have that I could share today. In Jesus' name, amen.

God First

*"First of all, look for the holy nation of
God. Be right with Him. All these other
things will be given to you also."*
Matthew 6:33

- - - - - - - - - - - - - - - - - -

Have you ever come down with a case of the Gotta-
Have-Its? "Mom, I've got to have _____." New
stuff can be exciting, but God doesn't want you to
spend all your time wishing for things. In fact, He says
that we don't even have to worry about having stuff—
He will give us everything that we need. Notice, He
doesn't say everything that we *want*. So, instead of
craving everything you could buy, look for God's way
of doing things. He wants you to do right, love others,
and be generous. Trust Him and pray about what you
need. He'll take care of you.

*Father, help me trust You and live for You. Today I
really need _____. In Jesus' name, amen.*

The Wrong Crowd

When you are around people who do not know God, be careful how you act. Even if they talk against you as wrong-doers, in the end they will give thanks to God for your good works when Christ comes again.

1 PETER 2:12

It feels good to fit in and have friends who like you. But be careful about trying to be accepted by other people instead of living like Jesus. Sometimes people can lead you to do wrong.

It's true, someone might laugh at you or dislike you for standing up for what's right. They might even say that you are the one in the wrong. But the Bible says to keep on being an example of God's goodness, kindness, and love with your actions and words. Maybe some of those people will even ask why you're different. And you can tell them how Jesus changed your life—and how He can change theirs too.

Heavenly Father, help me choose right, even if it means some people don't accept me. Amen.

One in a Million

All will be quiet before You, and praise belongs to You, O God, in Zion. And our promise to You will be kept. O You Who hears prayer, to You all men come.

PSALM 65:1–2

- - - - - - - - - - - - - - - - -

Sometimes life feels overwhelming. Your schedule can get jam-packed in a hurry. It's easy to start feeling small and overlooked in the chaotic rush of life. And maybe you're tempted to think that God isn't listening to your troubles when He probably has people with much bigger problems asking Him for help. But remember that God has no limits to His power and knowledge. God is different from you. He created you to be in one place and think about a limited number of things at a time, but it's no trouble for Him to hear millions of prayers and give each one His special attention. He's in all places all the time.

God, You're pretty awesome. I'm so glad that You can hear me over the crowd. Today I want to talk to You about _____. Amen.

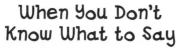

When You Don't Know What to Say

In the same way, the Holy Spirit helps us where we are weak. We do not know how to pray or what we should pray for, but the Holy Spirit prays to God for us with sounds that cannot be put into words. God knows the hearts of men. He knows what the Holy Spirit is thinking. The Holy Spirit prays for those who belong to Christ the way God wants Him to pray.

ROMANS 8:26–27

Have you ever been asked a tough question. . .and you just didn't know what to say? Sometimes we don't know how to tell God about our feelings either. But don't worry. The Bible says that when you belong to God, the Holy Spirit can help you out. He will pray for you in the way God wants Him to. If you're confused about things, pray about it, even if you don't know what to say. The Holy Spirit understands your heart.

Lord, today I'm not sure how to tell You how I feel about _____. Holy Spirit, please pray to God for me. In Jesus' name, amen.

Best Foot Forward

Whatever work you do, do it with all your heart. Do it for the Lord and not for men. Remember that you will get your reward from the Lord. He will give you what you should receive. You are working for the Lord Christ.
COLOSSIANS 3:23–24

- - - - - - - - - - - - - - - - - - -

You might wonder if it's okay to ask God for help when you know you've dropped the ball—like when you didn't study for a test or practice for your music lesson as much as you should have. You can talk to God about anything. But don't forget that He's not a magic eraser for poor decisions. He expects you to do your best. So study for your tests, and then pray for clear thinking, calm nerves, and the ability to remember the things you've studied. And ask God to help you make wise choices about how you spend your time and energy.

Heavenly Father, help me work hard and do my best so I don't have to ask You to rescue me from my poor choices. Amen.

What You Really Want

*Be happy in the Lord. And He will
give you the desires of your heart.*
PSALM 37:4

- - - - - - - - - - - - - - - - - - -

You really don't want to go to school tomorrow, so you pray for three feet of snow overnight. But then you wonder: Is God okay with that? God doesn't mind if you talk to Him about everything, but He also wants you to treat Him like the loving, powerful God and Father that He is. Learn to want the things that are important to God instead of treating Him like a vending machine to serve foolish and selfish desires. It's wise to go to school and learn, and it's good to obey your parents when they say it's time to go. As you learn to be like Jesus, you'll start wanting what He wants, and then the desires of your heart will come true.

*Heavenly Father, I know You love me a lot and
always know what I'm thinking. Help me learn wisdom
and pray for things that are pleasing to You. Amen.*

Pray for Missionaries

As you pray, be sure to pray for us also. Pray that God will open the door for us to preach the Word. We want to tell the secret of Christ. And this is the reason I am in prison. Pray that I will be able to preach so everyone can understand. This is the way I should speak.

COLOSSIANS 4:3–4

Missionaries need our prayers because they're doing important work telling others about Jesus and how He can change their lives when they love and obey God. But Satan likes to create problems and trouble to frustrate and discourage missionaries—like getting sick, jailed, or made fun of. Only God can change people's hearts, so pray that He'll open their hearts to the message that missionaries share. Pray that God will protect missionaries from Satan's attacks and keep them strong to do His work.

Lord, I want to pray for _____, who are serving You as missionaries. Keep their minds and bodies strong, and protect them from the enemy's attacks so they can tell more people about Jesus. Amen.

Brave One

"Be strong and have strength of heart. Do not be afraid or shake with fear because of them. For the Lord your God is the One Who goes with you. He will be faithful to you. He will not leave you alone."

DEUTERONOMY 31:6

- - - - - - - - - - - - - - - - - - - -

Have you ever had to face a bully alone? Scary, huh? But if a friend goes with you, suddenly your courage is boosted! The Bible tells us to be strong and have courage because God goes with us. Everywhere you go, God is always there with you. That's what it means to be faithful: to never leave. God is faithful to you—you'll never be alone! Sometimes we need to be brave to do the right thing—like helping out a friend or being kind—even when no one else is. God helped David bring down a giant, and He can help you too. Pray for courage to do the right thing.

Lord, give me strong faith like David's. Today I need courage to face _____. Amen.

Pray Your Life Will Honor God

Whatever you do, do everything to honor God.
1 CORINTHIANS 10:31

- - - - - - - - - - - - - - - - - -

Have you ever loved to do something—like playing soccer or dancing? If you're a soccer player, then you've probably spent a lot of time thinking about soccer, practicing soccer, and playing soccer games. Your soccer skills might be worthless to someone else, but in your mind they're priceless. Honor works the same way. To honor something or someone means you've given it worth in your life. To honor God means your life shows that He's valuable to you.

So how can you honor God with the things you do? You give Him value in your life by thinking about what He would want you to do. That means making the choice to do what the Bible says is right—not because your parents say you have to but because you think God is precious and a must-have in your life.

Lord, help all my choices show that I love You. Today I need help honoring You by choosing to _____. Amen.

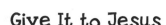

Give It to Jesus

He took the five loaves of bread and two fish.
He looked up to heaven and gave thanks.
He broke the loaves in pieces and gave them
to His followers. The followers gave them to
the people. They all ate and were filled.
MATTHEW 14:19–20

Do you feel small, insignificant, or maybe just young? Jesus met a young boy who gave Him his lunch. And with that little boy's lunch, Jesus fed over five thousand people—and they had leftovers too! Now, your lunch may not stretch that far, but Jesus can take whatever you offer Him and multiply it just like that food. You're not too young or unimportant to be used by God for big things. What talents do you have? Try giving them to God, and see what miracles happen.

Heavenly Father, I don't have much, but I
want You to use my talent for _____
to bring people to Jesus. I know that You can
do big things with small offerings. Amen.

Who Will You Serve?

"Choose today whom you will serve. . . . But as for me and my family, we will serve the Lord."
JOSHUA 24:15

Life is full of choices. Some don't really matter, like which flavor of ice cream you'll eat, but others can make a huge difference. You decide which friends to spend time with and what activities will fill your day. You choose to obey your parents or to disobey. You choose to be kind or rude with your words and actions. You choose whether to spend time reading your Bible. . .or not.

It's important to stop and think about who you're serving with your choices. Are you choosing to serve God by doing what is right and good? Or are your choices leading you into the enemy territory of sin? They may seem small, but all your little choices added up become your character. What are your choices saying about your character? Are you choosing things that please God?

Heavenly Father, help me choose to serve You today and every day. Amen.

Confessions of a Sinful Heart

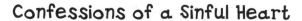

*The Lord will not hear me if I hold on to
sin in my heart. But it is sure that God
has heard. He has listened to the voice of
my prayer. Honor and thanks be to God!
He has not turned away from my prayer
or held His loving-kindness from me.*

PSALM 66:18–20

- -

Rest assured that God will always hear you. He even hears your thoughts. So whether you're thinking, whispering, or shouting, nothing can stop God from hearing your prayers. God loves you a lot—but never forget that He hates sin. So if you are keeping sin in your heart, He knows it's there (you can't hide it from Him). And He's waiting for you to acknowledge your sin first. God is always available. He never has you on mute. Is there any sin in your heart you need to confess today?

*Heavenly Father, I'm so glad I can talk to You anytime.
Today I need to confess to You _____ and
ask for Your forgiveness. In Jesus' name, amen.*

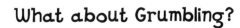

What about Grumbling?

O Lord, how long must I call for help
before You will hear? I cry out to You,
"We are being hurt!" But You do not save us.
Why do you make me see sins and wrong-
doing? People are being destroyed in anger
in front of me. There is arguing and fighting.

HABAKKUK 1:2–3

- - - - - - - - - - - - - - -

Does God mind if we complain to Him? If you read the psalms, you'll see that David and others in the Old Testament were totally honest with God about their feelings. (It's not as if you can hide how you're feeling from Him anyway.) They went to God when life seemed unfair, but they didn't blame God or say that He was wrong or not powerful enough to control the situation. Instead, they told God how they trusted in His goodness and perfect plan. God's on your side. Trust Him, and He will help you.

Lord, it seems unfair that _____.
I know You are powerful and good.
Please help me. In Jesus' name, amen.

Captured Thoughts

*Take hold of every thought
and make it obey Christ.*
2 Corinthians 10:5

- - - - - - - - - - - - - - - - - - -

You probably realize that all your actions—both right and wrong—start with a thought. The Bible tells us to be careful what we spend our time thinking about— and to catch all the wrong thoughts and lock them up, just like the police put the bad guys in jail so they can't cause trouble. Your enemy, Satan, is totally happy when you're thinking wrong thoughts. But you can beat him by asking yourself if a thought pleases God. If it doesn't, get it out of your head! Wondering why you should please God? The Bible says that Satan is here to steal and kill and destroy. He's not the kind of friend you want! But God loves you and is faithful to you. He's the best kind of friend.

Pray about your thoughts today. Would they make God smile? Or do they need to be locked up?

*Father, help me see when my thoughts are wrong,
and change them into right thoughts. Amen.*

The Freedom of Forgiveness

*A man's understanding makes him slow
to anger. It is to his honor to forgive
and forget a wrong done to him.*

PROVERBS 19:11

- - - - - - - - - - - - - - - - - -

The world around us is kind of hyped up on drama. Forgiveness isn't really that popular when gossip and being offended rule the day. But Jesus wants us to do things His way. And drama is definitely not it. His way is to overlook a wrong that's been done to us—to forgive. When someone hurts you, forgiveness can be tough. Remember, though: Forgiving doesn't mean that you think what they did was okay. It just means that you choose not to allow your hurt to make you sin by becoming angry or trying to get back at the other person. How you respond is your choice. Make the right one and respond with gentle words.

Pray about how you've been hurt. God understands your pain. Is there someone you need to forgive today?

*God, I really need Your help to
forgive _____. Amen.*

A Close Friend

*"I am the Lord, the God of all flesh.
Is anything too hard for Me?"*
JEREMIAH 32:27

How far away is heaven, and can God hear me from there? Have you ever considered that? We might not be able to measure a distance to heaven, but don't fall for the enemy's lie that God is somewhere "out there" far away and doesn't care about you and the problems you face every day. God is right here, living among us. He sent His Son, Jesus, to us—Immanuel, whose name actually means "God with us." You have a friend who is always close. And He says that nothing is too hard for Him—not even reaching out from heaven to help you with your struggles.

*Heavenly Father, sometimes I feel like You
are far away or that You're not interested in
the things that I'm struggling with. Help me
remember that You're actually close by. God,
today I need Your help with _____. Amen.*

Never Tired

*O Jacob and Israel, why do you say,
"My way is hidden from the Lord. My God
does not think about my cause"? Have you
not known? Have you not heard? The God
Who lives forever is the Lord, the One Who
made the ends of the earth. He will not
become weak or tired. His understanding
is too great for us to begin to know.*
ISAIAH 40:27–28

Sometimes your parents might tell you that their ears
need a break or that they need some quiet time, but
God never tires of your prayers. He loves you more
than anyone else. Jesus came to earth and died for your
sins so that you could be friends with God. He wants
to answer your prayers and work in your life by changing your habits and thoughts. Even if you pray for the
same thing over and over, you'll never wear Him out.

*Heavenly Father, I'm so thankful that You're always
listening and never tired of hearing from me. Today
I want to talk to You about _____. Amen.*

When You Need a Friend

Please have a room ready for me.
I trust God will answer your prayers
and let me come to you soon.
PHILEMON 22

- - - - - - - - - - - - - - - - - - -

Everyone feels lonely at times. Sometimes it seems like no one gets you or wants to be your friend. It's okay to ask God to send a good friend into your life. He loves you and wants you to have good friends. And He wants to comfort you when you're feeling sad. Be honest with your heavenly Father, and let Him know how you're feeling.

And maybe if you're feeling lonely, someone else is too. Being a good friend is a great way to have good friends. Pray that you could comfort someone else too.

Lord, I'm feeling lonely and disconnected from
everyone. I'd really like to have a good friend.
Help me see if there is someone around me
who needs a friend. In Jesus' name, amen.

Pray Like Jesus

"Pray like this: 'Our Father in heaven, Your name is holy. May Your holy nation come. What You want done, may it be done on earth as it is in heaven. Give us the bread we need today. Forgive us our sins as we forgive those who sin against us. Do not let us be tempted, but keep us from sin. Your nation is holy. You have power and shining-greatness forever. Let it be so.'"
MATTHEW 6:9–13

You might have heard of the Lord's Prayer. Jesus' disciples once asked Him to teach them how to pray. The Lord's Prayer is the example that He gave them. It's a great model to follow in your prayers and shows you what kinds of things God wants you to be praying for. Read it every once in a while, and it will give you ideas for your own prayers—like praising God for His greatness, thanking Him, and asking for needs.

Heavenly Father, thank You for teaching us how to pray for the things that are important to You. Today I want to pray about _____. Amen.

Scripture Index

OLD TESTAMENT

Check Out These Fun Faith Maps!

The Prayer Map for Girls
978-1-68322-559-1

The Prayer Map for Boys
978-1-68322-558-4

These prayer journals are a fun and creative way to fully experience the power of prayer. Each page guides you to write out thoughts, ideas, and lists. . . which then creates a specific "map" for you to follow as you talk to God. Each map includes a spot to record the date, so you can look back on your prayers and see how God has worked in your life.

Spiral Bound / $7.99